BACK ROADS LORE

THE WEIRD WILD WEST

LEWIS - WEATHERLY - NELSON

Published by

EERIE LIGHTS

Eerie Lights Publishing

Back Roads Lore: The Weird Wild West

by Lewis - Weatherly - Nelson

Based on travel, interviews, and research conducted by Back Roads Lore.

ISBN: 978-1-945950-48-3

Published by Eerie Lights Publishing, Florida, USA

Cover Art by Rick Fisk

Editor: Jerry Hajewski

Layout | Design: Digital Cricket
DigitalCricketDesigns@proton.me

Printed in the United States of America

Back Roads Lore
backroadslore.com

EERIE LIGHTS

eerielights.com

eerielightspublishing.com

TABLE OF CONTENTS

Features

Columns

Introduction

When we first started discussing themes for volumes of Back Roads Lore, we had plenty of ideas to focus on. One of the first topics that came up was a western centered issue. It's no surprise of course, after all, David has explored the southwest in depth, Kevin has a special love for South Dakota, and Chad… well, Chad thinks that Jackalope racing should be a national pastime.

This volume was both easy and challenging to compile—for the same reasons really—there are so many fascinating and strange stories in the west that it was hard to narrow the focus down to what would fit in a single volume. We had plenty to pick from, but we knew that we had to be selective. In the end, we decided to stick close to the idea of the *Weird* Wild West. Here you'll find topics not often covered, truly odd tales of Tommyknockers, the Jarbidge Giant, the monster of Elizabeth Lake and the aforementioned Jackalopes. There are ghosts aplenty, too, from the phantoms of Tombstone, Arizona, to the haunts of Deadwood, South Dakota, to Nevada's Lady in Red.

As usual, you'll also find our regular columns with great roadside stops, legends, dares and more—this time with a weird west theme as well. Grab your boots and let's hit the trails for some weird western lore.

— Back Roads Lore

J. COLLAR
CENTENNIAL
RESTAURANT
BOOT HILL

Behind This Curtain

Boot Hill Museum & Distillery

By Kevin Lee Nelson

"To any Traveler who may pass this way, and climb this lonely hill and say

A prayer for us who early found our rest upon the prairie's wind-swept ageless breast.

Weep not for us who early made our beds, wrapped in our blankets, saddles for our heads.

For we are happy here, secure and still, locked in this rock-strewn, silent, sun-baked hill."

— *Boot Hill* by Josephine McIntire

In 1865 Fort Dodge was founded in Kansas near the Arkansas River to protect wagon trains of settlers moving westward as they passed through tribal lands. Other settlers quickly recognized the benefit of setting up business near the fort. Besides protection, the site offered a steady stream of customers passing by along the Santa Fe Trail. By 1872, what was previously a ramshackle cluster of shops, livery stables, and saloons had become Dodge City.

In its early days, Dodge City was a rough and lawless town. Most local men didn't live to a ripe old age, as many were gunned down, killed in saloon brawls, or hanged from a gallows. The town's flourishing graveyard was the original "Boot Hill," getting its name from of all the men who "died with their boots on" in gunfights or at the end of a hangman's noose. Another tale states the "Boot Hill" moniker came about because the graveyard was mostly occupied by "drifters, troublemakers, and unknowns" who were buried in unmarked

graves. They were buried without coffins, so to give the poor souls a modicum of comfort, their boots were placed under their heads as pillows.

By 1878 the graveyard was already causing the town troubles, as the graves were frequently dug up by wolves. So, the city council ordered the bodies (roughly 34, give or take) to be removed. The bodies were relocated to a different location in Dodge City to make room for a public school built on the site. The school was then torn down about fifty years later in 1927 to make room for the current municipal building. Today the building has been updated and re-purposed into the town's new distillery, Boot Hill Distillery. The Boot Hill site has gone from being a place of buried spirits to a place of bottled spirits.

I spoke with one of the distillers while sipping a glass of their amazing whiskey. He said they are trying to create a whiskey that has a distinctly Kansan character. Kansas is known for being one of the biggest producers of wheat. So, utilizing a local and abundant resource, their new batch is 100% wheat, unlike bourbon or scotch. Sweet and complex. At cask-strength it packs a wallop. Dodge City is no longer a place where shots are fired; instead, today it's a place where shots are poured.

Did I mention the distillery is haunted? You see, when they moved the bodies from Boot Hill all those years ago they could never find one body: Ed Masterson, the brother of Wild West legend, Bat Masterson. He's still planted there somewhere, and now many claim his restless spirit haunts the distillery. Or is it just the whiskey talking?

BOOT HILL
DISTILLERY

Adjacent to Boot Hill is the Boot Hill Museum. It first opened in 1947 to preserve Dodge City's unique Wild West Heritage. Over the years historic structures have been donated and moved to the site, including an original Santa Fe Railroad Depot, a 1915 one-room school house, an 1880s blacksmith shop, and an old Catholic Church.

Part of the museum includes old Front Street, featuring recreated businesses like the Long Branch Saloon, Tonsorial Parlor, and an undertaker. Boot Hill museum displays more than 60,000 relics, photographs, and documents from the golden era of the Wild West, including a "Guns that Won the West" gun exhibit and a "People of the Plains" exhibit featuring artifacts and information about the area's indigenous people. Other exhibits include, "Forts and Railroads," "Buffalo Hunters," "Cattle Industry," "Santa Fe Trail," and a "Cowboy Hall of Fame" exhibit. And of course what tourist attraction would be complete without a fudge shop and gift shop full of Wild West souvenirs? The Boot Hill Museum has you covered on both.

If you find museum exhibits a bit too dull, and you prefer something a bit more lively, head over to Boot Hill Museum's Long Branch Saloon for their variety show. The Long Branch Variety Show is the longest running seasonal theatrical show in the nation — over 60 years! You can see song and dance numbers including ragtime piano tunes, Can-Can dancers, comedy routines, and enjoy a country style dinner.

The Boot Hill site, including the Boot Hill Museum and the Boot Hill Distillery, are a must-see for any fan of the Old West.

Boot Hill Museum
500 W. Wyatt Earp Blvd.
Dodge City, KS 67801

Phone: 620-227-8188
Email: info@boothill.org
Website: https://www.boothill.org/

The Mysterious Outdoors

Dead Horse Point State Park

By David Weatherly

Established in 1959, Utah's Dead Horse Point State Park features stunning overlooks of the Colorado River and Canyonlands National Park. The park, in San Juan County, spans 5,362 acres of high desert with its highest point at 5,900 feet. The park offers majestic views with twisting canyons and the Colorado River 2000 feet below the lookout points. To the southwest you can see Canyonlands National Park.

The park's unusual name relates to a long-standing legend—one involving the tragic death of some wild horses and their lingering phantoms.

In the late 1800s, wild mustangs ran free in the deserts of Utah, and plenty could be found along the mesa that is now known as Dead Horse Point. Sadly, for the animals, the top of the plateau was a natural corral that some cowboys took advantage of. A group of men decided to capture some mustangs, break them, and sell them for a profit. They wrangled a number of horses into the area and trapped them on a narrow point now known as the neck. This skinny area has dramatic drops on three sides and once the cowboys had pushed the animals out on the neck, they blocked off the end with a makeshift fence to eliminate the animals' only path of escape.

The cowboys took the horses they wanted and rode away, callously leaving the remaining horses trapped in the makeshift corral. Trapped in the pen and left without food or water, the poor animals starved to death on the point.

The most frequent paranormal reports are from people who say they hear the mournful whinnying of horses around the point itself. The sounds are often

heard at night, and believed to be from the ghostly equines trying to escape their prison. The echoing sounds are a chilling experience for those familiar with the tragic tale.

Campers and people exploring the area have reported hearing the thundering sound of hooves running nearby. Some people even claim they've seen phantom horses running along the mesa, finally making their escape and reclaiming their freedom.

When I was exploring the region myself in 2010, I met a woman named Sharon Butler who told me she'd heard the phantom horses. Sharon had her experience late one day in the summer of 2006. She and her then husband had spent the day exploring the park, hiking around, taking in the views, and enjoying the calm, pleasant weather. Nothing unusual occurred until they set out to leave the park. Sharon says they had dinner plans in Moab that evening, and they wanted time to clean up and change before meeting friends. She says that when they were leaving the park, a strong gust of wind suddenly came up. She recounts:

"It was just after four o'clock when we were walking out. We paused for a moment because of the wind. The day had been completely calm before that. The next thing I knew, I heard horses galloping. I'm confident that's what it was since I worked with horses for years. The sound seemed to come from the point and rush toward us. We stood there looking all around, expecting to see some horses. Another breeze came up and it sounded like horses ran by close to us, but we never saw a thing. The sound of their hooves faded away and everything got calm again."

There's no record of the incident to back up the legend, but the reports have continued to come in through the years, so much so that Dead Horse Point State Park is now known as the most haunted campground in Utah. As it turns out, phantom horses aren't the only spirits reported in the park. Some people have claimed to see the ghosts of native Americans in the area. Whether this is residual energy or whether it's the spirits of people from the past still wandering the region is anyone's guess.

Dead Horse Point State Park is located just over thirty miles from the town of Moab. The park has a visitor's center and there are campgrounds for those interested in spending more time exploring the area and the park's trails. In 2016, Dead Horse Point State Park was recognized as an International Dark Sky Park so it's a great place for stargazing and night sky photography, plus, you may catch a glimpse of some majestic, phantom mustangs.

Resources and Works Consulted:

Stateparks.utah.gov/parks/dead-horse/

The Elizabeth Lake Monster

By Chad Lewis

When we think of the wild west, most of the attention and scholarly focus goes to the iconic larger than life human characters. Tales of no-nonsense lawmen, deadly outlaws, unscrupulous gamblers, ill-tempered gunslingers, enthusiastic prospectors, and ladies of the night were the most interesting and entertaining legends of their time. Yet, hidden among these fascinating stories is a treasure trove of odd and perplexing monster legends that are truly beyond belief. Nowhere is this more apparent than with the Elizabeth Lake Monster.

The 1800s is one of the most interesting periods of time to research oddities. Over the years, I have done several books featuring some of the most bizarre and perplexing legends and lore that were chronicled by the newspapers of that time. If you are ever bored on a rainy day, I highly suggest you flip through the old newspaper archives where you will discover some of the weirdest tales of bizarre deaths, peculiar people, psychic phenomena, oddities, haunted places, and of course, mysterious creatures.

One of my favorite types of cryptids to research is that of sea serpents/lake monsters. If you have an interest in lake monsters, there was no better time in history to spot these beasts than in the 1800s. The newspapers of the era were chock-full of the most amazing and fantastical sightings that you can imagine. Subsequently, the lack of any advanced technology and modern science of the time often led to complete cluelessness when it came to mapping and exploring lakes.

In Minnesota's Lake Pepin, which has an average water depth of only 18 feet, researchers believed that the sea serpent sightings there were most likely caused by a giant whale swimming in the water. In Wisconsin's Brown Lake, researchers claimed the lake possessed a bottomless pit that the beast used as its hunting lair. Although we must take these older cases with a grain of salt, we recognize that for each example of an outrageously hoaxed case, we have an equally puzzling one to accompany it. Although it is called the Elizabeth Lake monster, this creature was nothing like the typical lake monsters of the day. In fact, by all accounts, this flying monstrosity appeared to be in the category of flying dinosaurs. The fact that it used the lake as its home base seems to be secondary. So buckle in because the legend of the Elizabeth Lake Monster might just have you flipping back and forth from believing it to be fact or fiction.

Elizabeth Lake sits outside of Los Angeles, California. Here is how an 1886 article in the *Ventura Free Press* described its location: "The old stage road from Los Angeles to Bakersfield runs through San Francisquito canyon and up by Elizabeth Lake, and to this day emmigrants (sic) coming from Nevada and the San Joaquin county to the coast in wagons follow this beaten track across the Mojave desert."

The Work of the Devil?

The Elizabeth Lake Monster is often referred to as the "Devil's pet" for good reason. The area surrounding Elizabeth Lake has long been thought to be cursed, as explained in the 1991 article of *The Signal,* which wrote, "More than 200 years ago the Spanish claimed that the long narrow slit through La Liebre Mountains was created by the Devil himself." *The Signal* newspaper expanded on the name's history, writing, "Long before the place was called Elizabeth it was known to the Spaniards, El Camino Del Diablo and La Laguna del Diablo---Devil's Highway and Lake."

The folklore of the area is rife with tales of those who chose to make camp along the shores of the deadly lake. It is said that for decades numerous ranchers and landowners, who believed that Elizabeth Lake was the ideal area to make their fortune simply uprooted and abandoned their property due to a never-ending streak of ill-fate. Mysterious fires would plague the area, often destroying entire ranches. Cattle and livestock that weirdly went missing were deemed to have been taken by the deadly monster dwelling in the lake. At night witnesses would hear the ear-piercing screams of the monster as it lurked just out of sight.

One legend of the land was explored in a 1985 article with *The Signal* newspaper which told of a party of Spanish explorers being confronted by a band of Native Americans in the fall of 1780. As the story goes, the Spanish reinforcements had become disoriented and lost until one of them cried out "that he would give his soul to the Devil himself for a road to the besieged Christians." The old adage of being careful for what you wish for applies here as the Prince of Darkness appeared and "pounded a highway directly from modern day Palmdale to Elizabeth Lake." When the time came for the soul to be delivered to the Devil, the Spanish refused and took up holding crosses to keep the Devil at bay. As the ground shook with fury, and fire and brimstone rained down on the men, they held tight to their faith (and their crosses). By morning the Devil was gone, and in his place was a large body of water. It is interesting to see how early peoples viewed the natural landscape of the area. Not knowing that the San Andreas Fault runs right under the lake and the peculiar odor that is released certainly could account for all the tales of a wicked brimstone smell permeating the area.

Tantalizing legends tell that once the Devil was expelled from the land, he placed the winged monstrosity in the lake to do his bidding. Locals would often half-jokingly claim that if you swam in the lake and dove to the bottom, you would discover a portal to Hell.

What was once only seen as foolish folktales and cautionary campfire tales took a sharp turn with the next encounter. Arguably one of the weirdest monster encounters occurred in 1886, when one traveling immigrant family headed up by Mr. Peter Simpson decided to take a respite from the dusty road and camp along the shores of the lake for the night. With them was their trusty wagon packed to the brim with all of their earthly belongings, a dozen head of cattle, and a boat load of optimism that this new land would provide a better life for them. However, as soon as darkness fell, the weirdness began. According to the *San Francisco Chronicle,* Mr. Simpson noticed a "peculiarly penetrating odor rising from the water." As if the unexplained scent wasn't bizarre enough, an undefinable mist began to blanket the area. Later that evening, as the family slept, Mr. Simpson was awoken by a "terrible commotion" emanating from the middle of the lake accompanied by an awful roaring. A groggy Simpson grabbed his loaded rifle and readied himself for whatever might be the cause of the disturbance. It was hard to make out anything in the darkness of night, but far out in the lake, he spotted a low black cloud hovering. Underneath the mysterious cloud the water was boiling, agitated by some powerful source. Finding himself in no imminent danger, and being used to any weather the land could throw at him, Simpson attempted to get some shut-eye, not knowing that in a few minutes all hell would break loose. Just as he settled back to sleep there "was a great rushing through the air as of mighty wings." Suddenly the family wagon was lifted into the air and carried for over 20 yards before being forcefully dropped back to the ground. The force of impact was enough to break apart the wheels and leave the wagon wrecked. As their cattle scurried away, the terrified family could only watch in amazement as a dark form buzzed about in the sky, the sounds of its beating wings growing fainter.

Rattled and shaken, Simpson's first thought was that his family had just survived a brutal cyclone. He "stood listening intently to the great silence which hung upon the desert." Off in the distance the eerie silence was shattered by a loud noise of conflict coming from the nearby darkness. Not easily spooked, Simpson followed the noise to the summit of a low knoll where he "gazed down into a little valley below him—and all over the scene fell a flood of warm summer moonlight." Apparently, the flying monster had bypassed the family and had homed in on a herd of sleeping antelope. The *San Francisco Chronicle* described the nightmarish scene like this: "about 10 feet from where Mr. Simpson stood a fine buck lay bleeding, bitten clean through at one stroke of the 'thing's' horrid jaws. Even more terrifying, the monster had folded its wings around another antelope and while its long tail, barbed at the end, played around in the air incessantly." Amazingly, the newspaper speculated that the wild whipping of its tail through the air was "evidently seeking to transfix" the struggling prey.

Whether this was a defense mechanism or some sort of hypnotic hunting talent, it seemed to have failed as several other antelope began gashing at the monster with their short horns.

Even more amazing than the beast's ferocious killing spree was how Mr. Simpson described its hideous appearance, saying, "It was about 30 feet long overall…and of a warm, reddish color, with a long snout and jagged yellow teeth. It had enormous wings rigged like those of a bat." It had long hind legs and a lengthy tail that ended with a hard barbed point. From its head and neck fell a shaggy mane. This last description might seem out of place for those who are not familiar with sea serpent sightings of the 1800s, but in actuality, a beast having a full mane of long shaggy hair or fur is quite common in the folklore literature. Undoubtedly, the scariest feature was the creature's large eyes that were said to have gleamed "like horrid fire."

After watching this dreadful scenario play out for over 10 minutes, Simpson, finally realizing that he might just be next on the creature's menu, took aim and fired a shot at the murderous beast. Unfortunately, the shot had no effect on the abomination as Simpson "heard the bullet strike and rebound." With a belly bulging with antelope, and a few still in its gaping mouth, the monster flew off toward the lake "where it sank with a splash that must have been audible for miles." The rest of the night was said to have passed without further incident, although it is hard for me to believe that Simpson or his family got any rest from that point on.

The next morning, under the safety and security of daylight, Simpson returned to the site of the previous night's carnage and gathered up an antelope carcass. He also discovered some scales that apparently had been ripped from the creature. The odd scales were described as being "round, semi-transparent, about the size of dinner plates, and of a reddish glazed appearance, somewhat similar to ground glass." Armed with proof of his unbelievable battle, Simpson journeyed into the nearby village of Carpinteria expecting to find an incredulous reception among the locals. Instead of experiencing ridicule and mocking, he was astonished to discover that several others also reported run-ins with the Elizabeth Lake Monster. The *Venture Free Press* even boasted that there was a young lady in town who had seen these scales as they were being put on display in Carpinteria.

I have to give credit to Mr. Simpson's superhuman powers of observation. In the pitch-black darkness of 1800s night, at a time when light pollution did not exist, after being tossed through the air like a Frisbee, he was able to perfectly capture the beast's physical dimensions from a fair distance away, even noting the color and shape of its teeth.

Strangely, by the end of the 1800s, stories of the predatory monster all but dried up. Some were convinced that whatever evil powers had led to its diabolical creation were finally removed, forcing the beast back to the fiery underworld from which it sprouted. Normally, this is where the tale would end. The story of the Elizabeth Lake Monster was relegated to snide skeptical remarks from nearby campers and tourists who brush off the legend as nothing more than fanciful 1800s beliefs. However, if oral tales are to be believed, the Elizabeth Lake Monster did not die, nor did it retreat back to Hades, it simply relocated to a less hostile land---and that land was Tombstone, Arizona.

The Tombstone Thunderbird

Elizabeth Lake is a bit over 500 miles from the town of Tombstone, Arizona—as the crow flies, or in this case, as the murdering giant winged monstrosity flies. You are probably asking yourself what the heck does the Elizabeth Lake Monster have to do with the Tombstone Thunderbird.

The Tombstone Thunderbird, sometimes referred to as a pterodactyl, is one of the most baffling and curious legends to come out of the Grand Canyon State. The wacky story goes something like this. On April 26, 1890, the local *Tombstone Epitaph* ran an incredible headline reading, “Found on the Desert A Strange Winged Monster Discovered and Killed in the Huachuca Desert.” The story told of two ranchers who were said to have encountered a giant winged monster that seemed to be “greatly exhausted by a long flight” or perhaps an intense hunting session, limiting its ability to fly away. “After the first shock of wild amazement passed,” the two men armed with Winchester rifles, perhaps worried that their friends and family would never believe such an incredulous sighting, diligently pursued the monster on horseback for several miles before they were able to get a clean shot at it. The wounded creature in a last-ditch effort for survival turned on the men, but “owing to its exhausted condition they were able to keep out of its way.” A few more well-placed blasts from their guns were enough to drop the beast once and for all. With the monster wounded, the men “cautiously approaching, their horses snorting with terror,” discovered that the beast was dead.

If things weren’t already beyond bizarre, here is where things get truly staggering. Upon measurement the creature was said to be over 92-feet in length, with its considerable girth being on display as it was over 50 inches in diameter. Just to give its thickness some perspective, a whiskey or wine barrel has an average diameter of 25 inches. Whatever this thing was, it was twice as

large as a barrel. Interestingly, the creature only had two feet "situated a short distance in front of where the wings were joined to the body."

The real mind-bending dimensions came when they were finally able to straighten out one of the monster's wings, which was "composed of a thick and nearly transparent membrane" measuring in at seventy-eight feet long. That is a total wingspan of nearly 160-feet! Again, just to compare this eye-popping size---the wandering albatross has the longest wingspan of any living bird, and it is only eleven and a half feet. Interestingly, neither of the enormous wings had any feathers or hair attached to them. The entire body was also devoid of any hair; instead, it was described as being "comparatively smooth and easily penetrated by a bullet."

The last paragraph of the article looked to entice the reader even further by reporting that the men had cut a piece of the monster's wing to keep with them and had plans to "bring the strange creature to this city before it is mutilated." Of course, as far as we know, the unveiling of the dead monster never came to fruition and nothing more on the matter was said.

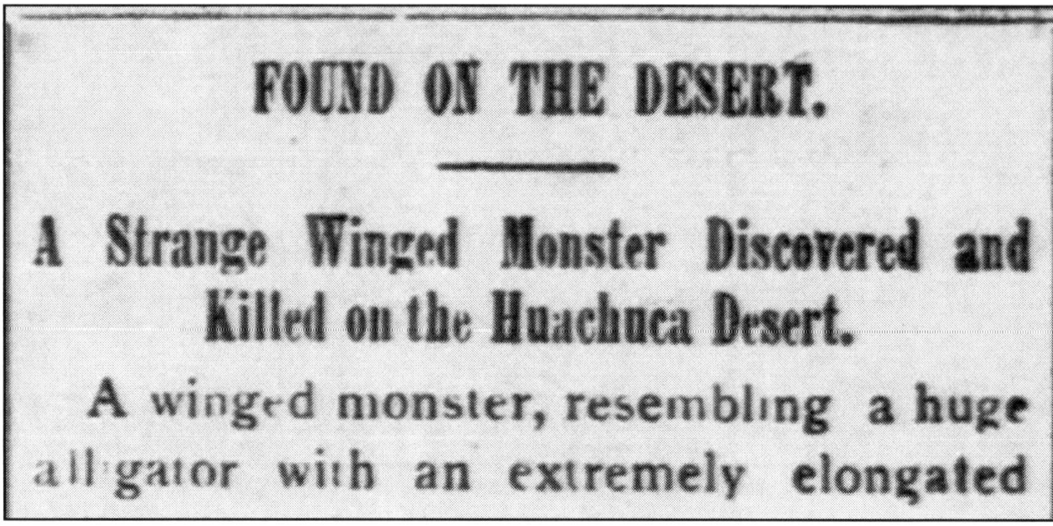

FOUND ON THE DESERT.

A Strange Winged Monster Discovered and Killed on the Huachuca Desert.

A winged monster, resembling a huge alligator with an extremely elongated

Believe it or not, the amazing story didn't send shock waves through the scientific community, and instead of celebrating the biggest potential scientific find of the century, the extraordinary tale simply drifted into oblivion and went forgotten for decades. In 1963, researcher Jack Pearl dredged the story from the ash heap of history for an article in *Saga* magazine.

If you can't imagine that the story could become any odder, you are sorely mistaken. Legend tells that not only did the newspaper recount the breathtaking encounter, it actually included a photograph of the monster as well. Numerous people were absolutely positive that they had personally laid eyes on the enigmatic photograph. The only problem with these assertions is that if a photograph was ever taken, no one has been able to locate it. The edition of the newspaper that carried the original story has no such photo on any of its pages. Here is where the story starts to meander into the Mandela Effect because a lot of people recall seeing a re-printed version of the original thunderbird photo in various other newspapers and magazines throughout the decades. Although one only needs to conduct a search online to find plenty of hoaxed photos of wild west men posing over the corpse of gigantic pterodactyl-looking monsters, no one has yet located the original photo in any format. Noted biologist and cryptozoologist Ivan T. Sanderson not only claimed to have seen the photo, he stated that he possessed a copy of it. Yet once again fate seemed to intervene as Sanderson was never able to produce the photograph.

What does the Elizabeth Lake Monster have to do with the Tombstone Thunderbird? As more and more researchers spent considerable amounts of time trying to track down the thunderbird photo, they began to notice some similarities between the two legends. Some find it too coincidental that a gargantuan bat-like creature that had been terrorizing the Elizabeth Lake area for decades suddenly disappeared from the area right before an eerily similar looking creature was discovered in the neighboring state. In addition to the timing working out, the physical descriptions of the two sightings do seem to mesh pretty nicely. Both were so monstrously oversized that the possibility of witnesses misidentifying them for any known animal becomes highly improbable.

Before we begin morphing these two creature sightings into the same beast, we do have to address some glaring differences. Remember, the Elizabeth Lake Monster was said to have a shaggy mane of hair or fur dangling from its head and neck area, while the thunderbird was thought to be completely devoid of all hair, feathers, or rough skin/scales. We also know that the Elizabeth Lake Monster had scale covered skin that could easily repel bullets, while conversely, the Tombstone beast's skin was extremely thin, seemingly providing no practical protection against gunfire---as evidenced by its being killed so easily.

I think a good amount of people believe the two creatures were one and the same by posing the question—what are the odds that there would be more than one of these colossal beasts lurking around in practically the same geographical location during the same time frame? Astute students of folklore will immediately recognize the fallacy of this belief. During the 1800s and early 1900s there were sightings of numerous giant flying beasts reported throughout the country. In 1902, residents living in Maryland were terror-stricken by sightings of a creature known as the Snallygaster. It, too, had immense bat-like wings and razor-sharp teeth and was reported to be able to snatch full grown humans or livestock into the sky. Reports varied on the effectiveness of weapons that were used to repel this creature. Some versions contend that a snallygaster was killed by bullets, while other sightings claimed the guns and bullets were essentially useless against the creature's hide.

For five nights in 1903, the small town of Van Meter, Iowa, was terrorized by a giant 9-foot flying pterodactyl-looking creature that had a large horn on its head and could project light onto those who spotted it. On several nights, townsfolk ended up shooting it with everything they had, which seemed to have no effect on the creature before it descended into an old abandoned coal mine. At the same time something weird was lurking in Van Meter, another humongous flying creature was encountered near Stansbury Island, Utah. Witnesses estimated the creature to be over 50 feet in length. This thing was so massive that it was seen easily flying through the sky with a full- grown horse in its mouth.

The most popular state park in Wisconsin is Devil's Lake. The early natives told amazing tales of the lake's origin, that the lake was formed when

the giant thunderbirds (Wakhakeera) engaged in a heated battle with the water monsters (Wakunja) who lived in a den in the depths of the lake. The great birds flew high above the land and hurled their thunderbolts down into the waters; the water monster shot up giant rocks and water spouts from the depths of the lake. The fight raged on for days. The effects of the battle ravished the land; trees were blown down, rocks were split open, and the land was torn up. Finally, the thunderbirds prevailed and journeyed back to their nest in the north. The list of other flying monsters goes on and on from the Jersey Devil of the Pine Barrens to the Native American thunderbirds throughout the entire Midwest.

Were any of the terrifying creatures the same one that was allegedly killed outside of Tombstone---probably not, but it illustrates that other weird winged creatures were out there and just because the timing and geography lined up, it doesn't provide anything more than some interesting speculation.

Before we jump to the conclusion that all of these sightings and legends come from a time when people were naïvely superstitious and without science and modern technology, there are numerous accounts of flying creatures that are larger than any currently known species. Take, for instance, the bizarre encounter/attack that occurred in the tiny town of Lawndale, Illinois, during the summer of 1977. Mrs. Ruth Loew told the *Moline Dispatch* that while she was busy cleaning the family camper, she heard "a scream from her son Marlan" who had been playing in the family's small backyard. She raced to the backyard to see what was wrong and arrived just in time to spot her son, "who weighs 70 pounds, battling a huge bird that was carrying him two feet off the ground." Perhaps frightened by the protective mother, the unknown bird dropped the young boy and flew off with another similarly sized bird. All of the noisy commotion caught the attention of the neighbors, James and Betty Daniels, who had been chatting outside with the boy's father. The threesome also caught sight of the giant birds that Ruth described as resembling black condors with "single white rings around their necks and eight-foot wingspans." Of course, a bird with an 8-foot wingspan is a far cry from the monstrous sizes of the Elizabeth Lake Monster and the Tombstone Thunderbird, but the case illustrates that there are still some flying beings today that are too large to fit into any of our known species.

After all the analysis and research, what are we to make of these seemingly outlandish claims of encountering such gigantic animals that are still unknown to science. To me, these stories are time portals back to the early days when entire belief systems were far different than they are today. They provide us an opportunity similar to walking into a historical museum and viewing a house that was lived in during the 1800s. The old furniture, decorations, and personal artifacts shine light on how life functioned in a different time. Do I believe that these witnesses actually encountered the beasts in the exact manner that was reported? Perhaps. But more interesting to me is what the engrossing encounters tell us about human nature, human belief systems, and how we function in a society. Regardless of what century we like to explore, humans are especially full of wonder and excitement with anything that breaks the everyday grind of life. For me, that is substantially more rewarding than whether or not a 100-foot flying dinosaur is truly coming after me. With that said, as I continue to roam the back roads, I hold out hope for the possibility that one of these extraordinary creatures might just be lurking around the next bend.

Resources and Works Consulted:

Lewis, Chad. *Hidden Headlines of California: Strange, Unusual, & Bizarre Newspaper Stories 1860-1910.* Unexplained Research Publications. 2016.

Lewis, Chad. *The Wisconsin Road Guide to Mysterious Creatures*. On the Road Publications. 2011.

Lewis, Chad & Voss, Noah. *Pepie: The Lake Monster of the Mississippi River.* On the Road Publications. 2014.

Moline Dispatch. July 28, 1977.

San Francisco Chronicle. July 27, 1886.

The Signal. October 26, 1991.

The Signal. September 6, 1985.

Tombstone Weekly Epitaph. April 26, 1890.

Venture Free Press. July 30, 1886.

Venture Free Press. August 6, 1886.

La Llorona

By David Weatherly

Ten-year-old Jose Garcia was playing near the river on his family's property in southern Texas one fall evening. The sun was setting fast, and the boy knew it was time to go home. He threw one last rock, skipping it across the water and watching it sink. He turned to walk home but a strange sound behind him caused him to turn around. Something was stirring the water close to the riverbank. At first, the boy thought perhaps it was a fish, but as he watched, something started to rise up from the water—a human figure—a woman to be specific. Clad in white, her long black hair obscured her face as she crawled onto the land on her hands and knees. The wide-eyed boy felt a chill come over him as he watched the figure. The appearance of the woman was disturbing enough, but there was a sound that came with her, a long, wailing moan that sent the terrified boy running as fast as he could back to his house. Jose had just encountered La Llorona.

Ask a half dozen people to explain La Llorona (pronounced "lah yoh-roh-nah") and you're likely to get six different answers. She's a wandering ghost, a spirit of vengeance, an unholy, trapped soul, a force of evil, a boogeyman, or rather boogeywoman, and more.

Known variously as the wailing woman, the weeping woman and the crying woman, the tale of La Llorona has deep roots.

Her story has been told for ages and she's long roamed around Mexico and the American Southwest. In fact, the story of La Llorona is one of the oldest ghost stories in the Americas.

In general, she's a ghostly figure, tall and thin. She was, and sometimes still is, described as a beautiful woman. She has long, flowing black hair and she is typically said to be dressed in white, with occasional stories depicting her in a black dress. But these are the gentler, ghostly versions of La Llorona. Other tales paint a very different and disturbing picture of the figure.

Christopher L. Rodarte, author of *La Llorona: Ghost Stories of the Southwest,* starts his volume on the legend off with this brief and creepy description:

"Wrinkled skin dripping with fetid water, twisting fingernails covered with black muck, wailing and gnashing of teeth—and unspeakable sin. These images haunt the imaginations of millions of people; they also are part of the bedtime stories many children will hear tonight."

This unnerving image, or a variation of it, is indeed one that many people have had impressed on them from the time they were children. And it has haunted them on some level well into adulthood.

Some depictions of La Llorona border even further on the monstrous, implying that she is perhaps something not quite human at all.

In 1968 American folklorist Bess Lomax wrote an article titled "La Llorona in Juvenile Hall" which contained reports of the weeping woman haunting a juvenile detention facility in California. Lomax notes that there were variations in the descriptions of La Llorona. By some accounts, she was young and pretty and dressed in all white or all black. Other reports referred to her as having long hair and wearing a hooded cape or veil over her face. Some of the stories said that she had the bones of her dead children embedded in her backbone.

La Llorona's appearance isn't the only thing that's unsettling about her manifestations. She's called the weeping woman or wailing woman for a good reason—it's due to their anguished cries that echo out when she's nearby. Sometimes the wail is "Ay, mis hijos!" or, "Oh, my children!"

Whatever one hears, be it a long wailing or a cry in search of missing children, those who know the legend say there's only one course to take upon hearing it—run away as quickly as possible and be sure to get away from the water.

Some versions of La Llorona make her an omen. In these cases, anyone who hears her wailing cries is doomed to die. This aspect of the spirit bears a clear similarity to the Celtic banshee, another omen of death.

The common thread among the various versions of La Llorona is that she is the spirit of a mother whose children drowned. Lost in grief, she now spends eternity searching for them along the rivers, creeks, and other bodies of water.

The history of La Llorona is lost in the fog of time leaving the origin of the strange spirit difficult to pin down. The earliest written reference to her comes from the 19th century sonnet by Mexican poet Manuel Carpio. Carpio identifies La Llorona as the ghost of a woman named Rosalia who was murdered by her husband.

The most common and well-known version of the La Llorona story says that she was a woman named Maria who married a rich Spanish gentleman. She bore him two children, usually reported as one boy and one girl.

When he was at home, Maria's wealthy husband paid her little attention, focusing only on the children. Despite having a family, the man continued to go out on the town leaving Maria home with the children.

The gentleman was popular with the local ladies, and one day, Maria spotted him out with another woman. In some perverse way, she blamed the children for her husband's affair, perhaps feeling that she had lost her beauty and appeal after giving birth, or perhaps resenting the fact that she had to stay home with the little ones.

Overwhelmed with anger, she took her two children to a nearby waterway and drowned them. After her terrible act, she was filled with regret and drowned herself. Days after Maria's death, La Llorona appeared at the spot where the children had died. The haunting figure cried out in the night, "Mis ninos, mis ninos!"

Legend says the crying woman is the spirit of Maria, stuck in purgatory and still wandering the world of the living to this day.

The madness that had taken over Maria also distorted her memories and she had forgotten what her own children looked like, leading her to search for any child she could find. Whenever she does come across a child, she takes the young one with her to a watery grave.

There are a few variations of the tale. One version says it's Maria herself who loved to drink and dance. Focused on having a good time, she forgot the children she left alone at home. In this version, the children either die by accident when Maria is out on the town, or, reminded of her responsibility she drowned the children to be rid of them. In both versions, the woman is still overcome with remorse and kills herself out of despair.

Later interpretations of the tragic story make the distinction that the father of the children was a wealthy Spaniard who abandoned his wife for a younger lover. Perhaps, some speculate, the children were killed as a way to get back at a wealthy man who had taken advantage of a native woman.

Still, the result of the actions is always the same, the woman is overwhelmed with grief, ends her own life, and returns as a mournful and vengeful spirit.

Decades of legend have resulted in various connections to La Llorona, and some researchers believe she's connected to a historical figure—a woman known as La Malinche, or Dona Marina.

Although she's commonly referred to as La Malinche, her birth name is unknown and there are other names associated with her, including Marina and Malintzin. She was a Nahua woman from the Gulf Coast of Mexico who is said to have contributed to the Spanish conquest of the Aztecs.

Dona Marina knew several native languages and she became an interpreter and guide for the Spanish leader Hernan Cortes. Dona Marina was said to be one of almost two dozen female slaves given to the Spaniards by the natives of Tabasco in 1519. Cortes reportedly took her as a consort and she later gave birth to his first son, Martin, who was one of the first Mestizos (a person of mixed European and native ancestry) born in the new world.

Although some accounts state that Dona Marina was a slave girl purchased by Cortes when he landed on the Mexican coast, she was purportedly a noble

Cortez—with Malinche acting as interpreter—meets Moctezuma II

woman who had been betrayed by members of her family and sold into slavery at the age of sixteen. This version actually makes more sense considering that she was apparently educated and fluent in several languages.

After the Mexican War of Independence which led to Mexico being free of Spanish control, La Malinche was portrayed as an evil figure, a symbol of treachery who betrayed the country to the invading conquistadors.

The view of La Malinche has shifted around a lot over the years and in the modern era she's a complicated figure. While at times she's still seen as a traitor, she's now often portrayed as the quintessential victim who had little control over the course of her life.

Overall, her connections to La Llorona seem questionable but she's not the only historical figure connected to the modern legend of La Llorona. Some researchers cast the origin of the weeping woman even further back and say she is a pre-Hispanic figure linked to traditional Aztec mythology, specifically to a character known as "The Hungry Woman" who constantly cries and wails for food. As Amy Fuller, lecturer in the History of the Americas at Nottingham Trent University points out, La Llorona's wailing is primarily nocturnal. Of course, this is only one of numerous distinctions between the two figures.

The bulk of the tales told about the La Llorona in the United States come from the Southwest with a heavy concentration from Texas, New Mexico and Arizona and along the United States/Mexican border.

Still, as the Hispanic people moved around and expanded to other places, the legend of the wailing woman went with them. Some trace her movements from across the border, around the southwest, and as far north as Montana where she reportedly lurks along the banks of the Yellowstone River.

"La Llorona will always follow, always," a Mexican friend named Luis told me. He elaborated, stating that the weeping woman would find Hispanic people wherever they settled because she is connected to the soul of their culture. "She will always be there to haunt new generations," he said.

Luis shared his own memories of the moment he first learned about the crying woman when he was a young boy. Leaning back, taking a breath, and shaking slightly, he recounted:

"I was about ten years old when my grandmother told me about La Llorona. My cousin and I were out playing, and we stayed outside longer than we were supposed to be."

Luis told me that his parents were away that evening and that only his grandmother was there to watch him and his cousin. It was well after dark by the time the boys went back inside the house. They were sure they would be in trouble for being out in the dark but Luis knew that his grandmother wouldn't spank them so they thought any punishment wouldn't be too bad. Little did he know that he would receive something worse than a spanking—something that would stick with him into adulthood.

Luis said that after he and his cousin went inside, his grandmother went and locked the door. She pulled back the curtain and looked outside as if making sure that nothing had followed the boys to the house. "It might be safe," the old woman said as she double checked the latch on the door and went to the living room.

Luis said his grandmother's actions sent a chill up his back as he now imagined all kinds of things outside in the darkness.

The boys were told to get cleaned up and changed for dinner. The three ate in relative silence and the old woman kept glancing around the room. At least twice, she got up, checked the locked door, and looked out of the window. Luis says that he and his cousin were too afraid to ask what was wrong. They were completely creeped out by the woman's behavior and all kinds of things were running through their minds.

The trio moved to the living room and when Luis tried to turn on the television, he was told to leave it off. The elderly woman, it seemed, wanted to be able to hear anything that might come around the house.

Finally, unable to bear it any longer, the boys asked the woman what she was so worried about. Luis recalls:

"She paused for a long minute, then she started to tell us about La Llorona. She described her in detail, the long black hair, pale skin like she was dead, and wearing a long white dress that was soaking wet and dripping water.

"She told us how La Llorona haunted the rivers and creeks and that she would come crawling out of the water at night. 'If she finds children, she drags them with her under the water,' she said.

"I was terrified. All I could think about was how my cousin and me (sic) had been playing down by the creek at the back of our property."

Luis says that he couldn't sleep that night and he stayed up worrying that La Llorona might be coming for him. He piled things up in front of his bedroom window in hopes of keeping her out and he was plagued by the image of the ghostly woman, dripping wet, climbing through the window.

"I didn't play down by that creek again for years," Luis says. "Even when I was well in my teens, I got a bad feeling whenever I went near that water because I always remembered my grandmother's story."

The Legends of America website references an interesting story from a New Mexico man named Pete Sanchez who had a startling encounter in Texas.

Sanchez was in the town of East Bernard, located in Wharton County southwest of Houston. The man had his radio blasting as he drove along on an otherwise normal day. As he was crossing the San Bernard River Bridge he was shocked by the sudden appearance of an apparition in the passenger seat of his vehicle. The semi-transparent woman was dressed in all black with a black lace veil over her face. The terrified Sanchez reacted by slamming the gas pedal down and speeding down the road. Once he was off the bridge, the driver glanced back at the passenger seat only to find that the ghostly woman in black had disappeared, and he was again alone in the vehicle.

Sanchez's tale harkens back to an earlier story from New Mexico involving the Garcia brothers—Epifanio, Carlos and Augustine. According to the tale, Epifanio had a heated argument with his parents and as a result, he and his brothers decided to leave the family's ranch in Ojo de La Vaca. The trio took a wagon and headed out for Santa Fe, but they didn't get very far. As they were traveling, a tall woman dressed in black with a black veil over her face suddenly appeared on the buckboard, sitting between two of the boys in the front of the wagon. The woman was silent, but her presence was so disturbing that Epifanio turned the horses around and headed back to the family ranch. Once the Garcia brothers were enroute back to their home, the woman spoke a single sentence—"I will visit you again someday when you argue with your mother."

Judith Shaw Beatty recounts a curious 1984 incident in her book *La Llorona: Encounters with the Weeping Woman*. The story was reported by a Santa Fe resident named Cosme Garcia.

Garcia was listening to police officers on a shortwave radio one night and was surprised to hear an unusual exchange. A woman had phoned the police station to report that she could hear La Llorona crying by the Santa Fe River.

Several police units and sheriff's deputies went to the scene and did a search, likely thinking that someone was in trouble. Garcia reports:

"I sat there for about a half hour listening to the transmissions—it was really something. They'd hear crying by a tree, and they'd go over there and there wouldn't be anything. Then they'd hear it from somewhere else, and they'd all run over there, and of course there wouldn't be anything there either. They were saying it sounded like a baby crying."

Amidst the mad rush of trying to find the source of the strange crying sounds, one officer announced over the radio, "We're never going to find her because it's La Llorona."

Reportedly, after this statement, the officers left the scene and nothing else came of the incident.

Over time, the list of the weeping woman's targets has grown but most commonly she's said to target misbehaved children and people who cheat on their spouses. She's also become a part of modern lore in other unusual ways. Purportedly, it's possible to summon La Llorona. This is done by sitting in a room with mirrors on all the walls, lighting a red candle, and repeating the weeping woman's name. Of course, no one seems able to point to a good reason

A modern representation of La Llorona photo by Carlos Galvan (via creative commons)

one would want to summon La Llorona in the first place, and the method sounds suspiciously similar to the process used to call forth the infamous Bloody Mary.

The legend of La Llorona is one that has passed from generation to generation and today, many Hispanics who grew up hearing the tales, and fearing the dreadful crying woman, still believe she's out there, haunting the waterways, waiting to embrace her next victim. Over time, the list of the weeping woman's potential targets has grown. Most commonly she's said to target misbehaved children, lost kids, or children who directly disobey their mothers. She's also known to come after people who cheat on their spouses.

La Llorona has appeared in various forms of media over the years including the 1953 Roberto Gavaldon film *La Llorona* and the box office hit *The Curse of La Llorona* from 2019. She's also now represented at Day of the Dead celebrations and there are even Halloween costumes of La Llorona.

On the surface, it might seem easy to simply dismiss the legend of La Llorona as a bit of strange folklore, a campfire ghost story, or simply a boogeyman, but to disregard the tales wholesale is a mistake. The stories are a deeply rooted part of the cultural fabric of both a people and a region. In true organic fashion, the tales have morphed and grown, and their territory has expanded.

It's not just Hispanic people that believe in La Llorona. Those of mixed heritage, Native Americans, even Anglos who live in the southwest are aware of, and in many cases afraid of, the weeping woman. Perhaps it's the result of the stories being so prominent for so many years combined with the conviction of belief of numerous generations of people in the region.

One thing seems sure, she will continue to be there near the water, waiting and watching. As my friend Luis told me: "She's there, always, always there by the water even though she doesn't always reveal herself. She looks for children, for people who have hurt children, and for people who have been unfaithful in their marriages. Be honest, be true and don't take a chance because La Llorona will come for you."

Resources and Works Consulted:

Beatty, Judith Shaw. La Llorona: Encounters with the Weeping Woman. Judith Beatty, Inc. 2019.

Fuller, Amy. The Evolving Legend of La Llorona, History Today, November 2015.

Hawes, Bess Lomax. "La Llorona in Juvenile Hall." Western Folklore Vol. 27, No 3, July 1968.

Legends of America website. Legendsofamerica.com

Rodarte, Christopher L. La Llorona: Ghost Stories of the Southwest. Ghost River Images, Tucson, AZ. 2019.

Modern day La Llorona photograph by Carlos Galvan (converted to B&W) via creative commons license CC BY-SA 4.0 Deed | Attribution-ShareAlike 4.0 International | Creative Commons.

The Red Ghost

By Kevin Lee Nelson

The Terror in the Desert

Of all the wild and peculiar tales the southwest has to offer, few are as bizarre as the legend of the Red Ghost. It all started in 1883 when a mysterious beast wrecked the tents of two Mexican gold prospectors that had been panning for gold in a creek near the San Francisco River. They woke in time to hear the galloping of heavy hooves and a terrible shriek. They were able to get out from under their collapsed tents in time to see something "taller than two horses" tear off into the brush. They tried following it and found strange tracks in the creek bed and saw where the brush had been trampled down by a huge beast, but they eventually lost the tracks among the rocky hills.

A few days later a "reddish beast" attacked and trampled a woman to death near Eagle Creek in southeast AZ. The woman was gathering water from a stream when a beast tore through a fence and attacked her. Her sister heard her screams and ran out of their cabin in time to witness the attack. Even stranger, she claimed that the crazed creature had a skeleton strapped to its back. She was too terrified to help. Instead, she grabbed the children and barricaded their cabin until the men returned later that night from tending their flocks. After hearing her story, the men took their guns down to the creek where they found the unfortunate woman "trampled and crushed as though a troop of cavalry had run over her." Later, when the coroner arrived, the surviving woman was asked to describe the creature. She said it was reddish, very tall, and "ridden by the Devil."

The beast was spotted a few more times only to quickly disappear back into the desert hills. One man said he had followed it to the edge of a high precipice. He thought he had it cornered, but when he approached, it galloped right off the cliff. He said it galloped straight across the valley to another cliff a half mile away. When pressed for more details he said he was positive it had not flown, but had galloped through the air 400 feet above the desert floor. However, readers should keep in mind that this same individual also claimed to have encountered a flying bear in New Mexico's Mogollon Mountains and also discovered a mountain of solid gold, but was driven away by Apaches, and conveniently could never find his way back.

The next person to see the strange creature was a hunter named Si Hamlin. He came over a ridge and saw a very large animal moving through the chaparral. It was about half a mile away, and once it moved into a clearing he recognized it as a camel. He only had a few moments to study it before it disappeared back into the brush, but he said the animal had a grisly burden on its back that looked like a man.

A few months later a rancher spotted a creature and recognized it as possibly a camel. Like the others, he noticed there was something weird about it. Strapped to the animal's back was something that looked like the skeleton of a man. He knew it had to be the same beast that killed the woman at Eagle Creek, but when he tried to get nearer it took off into the desert. The dangerous animal was accused of all sorts of depredations and locals became afraid for their lives. As rumors and sightings continued, the rust-colored camel and its skeleton rider became infamous throughout the region. Everyone began to whisper and speculate about what they called the *Red Ghost.*

Camels in the Southwest?

You're probably wondering: *How did a camel find its way to the American southwest in the 19th century?* Most historians believe the Red Ghost was one of the camels the US Army had tried to introduce to the southwest when it began the Army Camel Corps in 1855. The Army wanted to develop a supply route through the southwest from Texas to California and thought the animals would be well suited pack animals for the arid southwest desert climate. Camels will also eat all kinds of prickly desert plants that most horses and mules won't touch. They could travel faster, climb rugged mountainous conditions, and survive much longer without water than horses.

It all seemed like the perfect solution. However, the experiment wasn't without problems. Many trainers didn't have enough experience working with the animals and the camels were often ill-tempered and difficult to work with. Unfortunately, this led to terrible mistreatment of the animals.

Cavalrymen viewed them as an abomination and mule drivers hated them because they saw the camels as a threat to their job. Camels also gave off an odor that spooked horses and mules. What finally brought a swift end to the experiment was the Civil War. Troops were withdrawn from the Southwest to fight in the East, and the Camel Corps was disbanded in 1863. Many of the animals were simply abandoned and allowed to escape into the desert. Others were auctioned off or simply shot. For years people would report seeing camels wandering around the Gila and Colorado rivers.

It is believed that the mistreatment and cruelty to the animals is what turned the Red Ghost into a killer. Camels are often seen as semi-docile pack animals, but if they are mistreated they can become extremely violent, and even become killers. In 2014 a man was killed by a camel at a monkey sanctuary in Tulum, Mexico. The camel savagely kicked and bit trainer Richard Mileski, and when he was almost dead, the animal sat on him until he was asphyxiated. In 2022 a rampaging camel trampled and killed two men after escaping from its enclosure at Shirley Farms Petting Zoo in Tennessee. In 2023 a camel in Rajasthan, India, rampaged, attacked its owner, and bit off his head. Adult male camels can weigh up to a ton and can run up to 40 miles per hour. The formidable animals can fit a person's head, arm, leg, or torso into their mouths and easily crush them. Considering their size, potentially explosive rage, and the fact that camels were very strange and unfamiliar to most people in Arizona in the 19th century, it's no wonder the Red Ghost was so feared.

US Camel Corps, 1857

The Skeleton Rider

Over the next few months stories of the Red Ghost grew to legendary proportions as it was encountered by terrified witnesses throughout the territory. Mexicans in the area even had their own name for it. They called it *Fantasia Colorado*. The next sighting of the Red Ghost was by a party of prospectors on a mesa near the lower reaches of the Verde River in the early morning as the creature fed. Two of them then crept up to it within shooting distance. They fired together, but even though they were both accomplished marksmen, they both missed. Startled, the Red Ghost dashed off, and as it did, the men saw something tumble to the ground, which turned out to be a human skull with bits of dried flesh and hair still clinging to it.

A few weeks later a cowboy from the Anchor-J ranch rode up to an abandoned branding corral. Immediately he noticed there was something odd in the corral. Before he even had time to register what it was, the Red Ghost came bursting out of the corral and charged the man and his horse. The cowboy managed to lasso the camel, but he immediately regretted it. The camel rammed right into the horse, and all three went down. Fortunately for the cowboy, the camel didn't stay to fight. It took off into the desert with 60 feel of rope trailing behind it. When he got back to camp he told the story about his encounter with the Red Ghost and what he saw on the beast's back. He said the pack on its back was nearly gone, but there was no question that it had once been a man.

The Red Ghost was probably spotted again here and there over the next few years as it roamed the Arizona desert, but by this time the human remains on its back would have finally fallen away. Without its skeleton rider the Red Ghost would have looked almost indistinguishable from other army camels that had escaped and were sometimes seen wandering the desert. In fact, wild camels continued to be spotted up until 1907. The last wild camel died in a California zoo in 1934. Perhaps once the Red Ghost was finally free of its burden the poor animal calmed down and became less dangerous, as no further attacks were reported.

But who was the unfortunate rider? Was he alive or dead when he was strapped to the camel? A number of theories circulated at the time. One claimed that the rider was a lost soldier weak with thirst who had bound himself to the camel in the hope it would eventually lead him to a watering hole or civilization. But he never made it. It sounds plausible, but others pointed out that the bindings were tied in such a way that there was no way he could have done it by himself. Nor could he have un-knotted the straps, so it seems he had been put in that unfortunate position by someone else. It was speculated that he must have been tied to the camel by another white man, as local Native Americans would have never wasted the supply of camel meat. Further theories suggested that the gruesome spectacle was revenge for some wrong doing and the man was intentionally condemned to a slow and agonizing death out in the desert. Yet others figured that perhaps it was a creative way of disposing of a corpse to eliminate incriminating evidence. The identity of the unfortunate rider and how his fate led him to be tied to a camel will always remain a mystery.

The End of the Legend

Finally, in 1893 the Red Ghost made one last appearance. A rancher named Mizoo Hastings woke to find the Red Ghost grazing in his garden near the Oro mining camp in what is Greenlee County today. He dropped the fabled beast with one shot from his Winchester. By this time the withered corpse had long fallen away, but the unfortunate camel still bore the traces of its ghastly rider. Hastings said, "The animal's back was heavily scarred from rawhide strips that had been used to tie down the body of a man. Some of the leather strands had cut into the camel's flesh." Who knows how long the poor animal wandered the desert with a dead man lashed to its back. Presumably, its macabre burden drove it mad and caused it to act out violently. The conclusion of the legend states that after shooting the creature, Mizoo Hastings tanned the hide and made boots out of the Red Ghost. So even after death the Red Ghost continued to walk the desert.

Resources and Works Consulted:

Anderson, Dorothy Daniels. *Arizona Legends and Lore*. 1991.

Cook, James E. "The Riddle of Red Ghost Tormented Ranchers". *The Arizona Republic*. April 7th, 1988.

Faulk, Odie B. *The U.S. Camel Corps: An Army Experiment*. 1976.

Froman, Robert. "The Red Ghost" *American Heritage*. Volume 12, Issue 3.1961

Lesley, Lewis Burt. *Uncle Sam's Camels*. 1929.

Parker, Lowell. "Red Ghost's Rider Remains Unknown." *Arizona Republic*. Decemeber 6th, 1978.

"The Phantom That Terrified All of Arizona for a Time." *Mohave County Miner*. February 25, 1893.

Weatherly, David. *Copper State Monsters: Cryptids & Legends of Arizona*. 2019.

Legend of the Jackalope
By David Weatherly

While some may argue that the American bison is the most iconic animal of the American West, there's another, stranger creature that could be a contender—the jackalope.

The name jackalope comes from a combination of a jack rabbit and antelope. In appearance, the creature looks like a large jackrabbit with a set of antlers. Despite the antelope comparison, the creature's horns more typically resemble those of a deer. The creatures are a bit bigger than normal rabbits.

Some stories claim that the jackalope was first seen in the 1800s by John Colter, the first known white man to enter the land that is now the state of Wyoming. There are also claims that Native American people in the region knew about the jackalope.

Other accounts claim that a man named Roy Ball discovered the creature when he was trapping in the region in 1829. In fact, a document hanging up at Douglas City Hall notes that Ball was the first human to officially lay eyes on the jackalope species. The document also mentions Ball being the "occasionally sober trapper" who owned the LaBonte Hotel.

Roy Ball did play into the legend of the jackalope, but it wasn't by spotting one in the 1800s. The creature's origins can be traced back to the early 1930s and a pair of teenage boys living in Douglas.

Brothers Ralph and Douglas Herrick had learned taxidermy via a mail order course, and they had a small shop on the family property where they did their work. One late afternoon in 1932, after a long day of hunting, the boys returned home and laid a jackrabbit down on the floor of their shop. By chance, it was placed next to a set of antlers from a previous hunt. In that moment, the antlers looked like they were on the rabbit's head and the Herricks were inspired. They mounted the rabbit with a set of antlers and the first jackalope taxidermy was created.

The unusual mount caught the attention of a man named Roy Ball, yes, the same one mentioned above. Ball purchased the jackalope mount for ten dollars and displayed it in his LaBonte Hotel downtown. The strange animal was quickly a talking point for locals and visitors alike and jackalope heads began to be in demand.

A taxidermy mount is one thing, but the legend of the jackalope became much, much more than a simple display, and plenty of curious folklore sprang up about the creature.

Jackalopes are said to be reclusive by nature and are rarely seen by humans. Weekends are the best time to spot the creatures, but even under the best conditions, finding them is difficult. Part of this may be due to their speed—the creatures are said to be able to run at an astounding ninety miles per hour—so fast that it's said when one runs by, there is nothing to see but a lingering trail of dust in the air along its trail. With such remarkable speed, one might assume that the animals are completely impossible to catch, but willey westerners discovered the jackalope's weakness, namely, it's favorite drink—whiskey. Like other rabbits, jackalopes have a keen sense of smell. Because of this, they can pick up the smell of whiskey from far away and more than one jackalope hunter has used a good single malt to lure the creatures into a trap.

Despite how many mounted jackalopes turn up in places like Douglas, the creatures may be endangered. You see, they only mate during thunderstorms!

But wait, there's still more weird jackalope lore. Lest you think that people are after the creatures just to create a fancy mount, jackalopes are even more desired because of their milk. Reportedly, milk from the jackalope is a veritable magical potion able to cure almost any illness affecting man, woman, or child. Adding to its medicinal properties, jackalope milk is purported to be an aphrodisiac, making it desirable for a whole different market.

Such a powerful cure all may sound appealing, but obtaining the milk, well, that's a whole different matter. As you would imagine, jackalopes don't simply let someone wrangle them down and swipe their milk.

Plenty of people have purportedly tried to catch jackalopes for a variety of reasons. The creatures are said to be very aggressive when cornered and they use their antlers in a defensive manner, poking and jabbing with the sharp ends.

Someone along the way proposed the idea that anyone attempting to catch a live jackalope should wear stovepipes on their legs to protect themselves from the creature's antlers.

Perhaps the most unusual trait that jackalopes have is the uncanny ability to understand the human language. Not only can they understand it, but they can also imitate it! Jackalopes have been known to repeat phrases back to humans in the way that parrots do. When pursued, the creatures use this ability to elude humans but shouting out phrases such as "He's over there!" and "He went that way!"

Not only can jackalopes speak the human language, but they can also sing. In fact, they're known for having excellent tenor voices. Legend says that in the 1800s, when cowboys would set up their camps at night and gather around the campfire on dark Wyoming nights, jackalopes would sit in the darkness outside the glow of the fire listening to the camp songs of the cowpokes. The jackalopes would sing back to the cowboys, repeating the songs they had learned from the humans. Sometimes they would even join in as the cowboys sang.

Some experts claim that jackalopes live in packs scattered around the Wyoming and South Dakota wilderness. According to Helga Bull, aka "the jackalope lady" of the Douglas Visitors Center:

"We do know that jackalopes roam together in groups of ten to twenty individuals. Scientists call this kind of group a 'committee' of jackalopes" (Branch, *On the Trail of the Jackalope*).

The creatures are said to be especially fond of the shortgrass plains found in Niobara County, Wyoming, and they are also frequently spotted in the sagebrush basins of central and southwest Wyoming as well.

But is the jackalope purely a fictional creature? While the Herrick brothers clearly had a hand in building the legend of the jackalope, there may actually be some truth to the idea of horned rabbits. There's speculation that early westerners could have spotted rabbits infected with a strange virus, one that causes odd growths on the face, around the ears and on the head of infected rabbits. In some cases, and especially from a distance, these growths can resemble horns.

Plate XLVII of Animalia Qvadrvpedia et Reptilia (Terra) by Joris Hoefnagel, c. 1575 depicting a "horned hare"

The virus, known as the Shope papilloma virus, or "SPV" for short, is a cancerous infection. The virus was named for Richard E. Shope, an M.D. who first described it in a scientific journal in 1933. Shope had examined infected wild cottontail rabbits that had been killed by hunters in Iowa. Cases of the virus were later confirmed in Kansas and the animals had numerous protuberances on several parts of their bodies. Shope noted that the protuberances resembled horns. The rabbits were commonly known as "horned rabbits" or "warty rabbits."

But even before Dr. Shope chronicled the weird ailment, there were records of horned rabbits over in Europe. Early folklore mentions the "lepus cornutus" or "horned hare," a creature depicted in both Medieval and early Renaissance texts from the 16th, 17th and 18th centuries.

"Lepus Cornutus" from the Historiae naturalis de quadrupetibus libri, 1655

In early texts, the creatures were sometimes real and sometimes mythical. According to Conrad Gessner's *Historiae Animalium*, horned hares were real animals that lived in Saxony. Persian art from the 13th century also depicts horned rabbits and they show up in 1575 in a piece by Flemish painter Joris Hoefnagel.

Another horned rabbit was said to live in Germany, specifically in the alpine forests of Bavaria and Baden-Wurttemberg in Southern Germany. This beast was known as the "wolpertinger." The wolpertinger was a mixture of several different animals including the rabbit, deer, squirrel, and pheasant.

The famous jackalope head that started it all, the one on display in the

LaBonte Hotel, was stolen in 1977. The unknown culprit was never caught and the jackalope was never recovered. The theft of the display only seemed to create more interest in the mythical figure.

As the legend of the jackalope spread, demand for taxidermy specimens rose. Demand became so high that the Herrick brothers could barely keep up with orders. Douglas eventually quit, purportedly after he and his brother had made around 1,000 jackalope heads.

Douglas passed away in 2003 at the age of 82. He had grown up on a ranch near Douglas, served as a tail gunner during World War II and worked at a refinery until his retirement in 1980. His legacy in jackalope lore lived on through his brother and his descendants who continued to make taxidermy mounts of the creature.

The family has many stories to tell about their years in the business. Ralph Herrick recalled speaking to a man from California—one wearing a Hell's Angels' motorcycle jacket. The man told Herrick that he wanted to catch some jackalopes so he could start a breeding farm.

You may think it was a tongue in cheek incident, but Herrick says the man was completely serious about his plan. Herrick informed the biker that jackalopes could only be hunted in the winter and the fellow went on his way. "Luckily, he hasn't been back. People get real mad if you tell them there's no such thing as a jackalope. They take it very seriously. And why make people mad?" (cityofdouglas.org).

Ralph Herrick and his son Jim ran the business for a time. During this period, Jim made multiple trips to the historic Wall Drug in South Dakota to deliver jackalopes. The store, famous around the world, has long been one of the biggest outlets for jackalope sales and Jim made so many trips to the location that he was nicknamed "Jackalope Man."

Jim ran the business for thirty-two years and today, the Herrick family continues to honor its jackalope legacy through Jim's son Luke who runs Herrick Big Horn Taxidermy. He creates several hundred jackalopes a year.

Over the years, the strange horned rabbit has become a quickly recognized creature. As the *Cowboy State Daily* notes:

"The jackalope has become a more relatable creature in recent years, as cartoon 'Jack' and 'Hare-iette' characters can be found plastered on walls throughout the city and on an I-25 billboard, beckoning people to come visit the city of 6,350 residents. Jack can often be found draped in a sleek red jacket or blue overalls, and Hare-iette usually has a red bandana wrapped across her furry brow. Neither can be found without a smile stretched across their faces" (June 11, 2023).

Over the decades, numerous attempts have been made to designate the jackalope Wyoming's official mythical animal. To date, the measure has not passed, but those behind the bill say they will keep trying until it is approved.

Today, Douglas, Wyoming, is proudly known as the "Jackalope Capital of the World." They've embraced the legend fully and each year in June, they celebrate the creature with the annual Jackalope Days Celebration.

Shops around town are filled with jackalope souvenirs including everything from t-shirts and hats to coffee cups, buttons, stickers and everything else jackalope themed that you could imagine.

The town also offers jackalope hunting permits but be aware, the license has some restrictions. The permit is only good for "one pronghorned jackalope of either sex." The larger sabretooth jackalope is off limits. Jackalope hunting season is short—they may only be hunted between midnight and 2 a.m. and only on June 31st. Yes, you read that right. Double check your calendar if you don't get the joke right away.

"Luke Herrick remembers a New York tourist obtaining one of the jackalope licenses and heading out to the hills with a shotgun in hand with the very real hopes of walking away with one of the horned rabbits. He was sorely disappointed when a Game and Fish warden cut his hunt short. 'Boy, was that guy mad,' Luke Herrick said" (*Cowboy State Daily*, June 11, 2023).

The town's original jackalope statue was on display downtown for a long time before an incident on Jackalope Day, May 19, 1984. The statue, built in 1965, became the victim of roadkill when it was struck by a drunk driver. When the local deputy showed up in response to the call, the man claimed that a big jackalope had jumped out in front of his truck.

The town quickly rallied and on Jackalope Day the following year, a new statue was erected. This one was eight feet in height and was soon shadowed by a thirteen-foot tall jackalope perched on a hill overlooking the town. This one was only a silhouette though and locals wanted something more significant. In 2007, the city purchased another jackalope statue; this one, almost twice the height of its nearby relative, sits in front of the Douglas Railroad Interpretive Center.

Although he wasn't horned, it's curious to note that among many Native American tribes, especially in the southeast, the rabbit is a trickster figure much like the western coyote.

The modern jackalope is ultimately more like P.T. Barnum's infamous Fiji Mermaid, a trick in and of itself designed to fool the masses.

Of course, the Herrick brothers deserve a good portion of the credit in the jackalope legend, but as the idea took hold, plenty of others added to the lore along the way and the folklore surrounding the beast grew. It now holds a unique place in both legend and pop culture, a creature that is both fantastic and absurd, yet is so firmly ingrained that many people believe it has to exist.

Resources and Works Consulted:

Branch, Michael P. *On the Trail of the Jackalope: How a Legend Captured the World's Imagination and Helped Us Cure Cancer*. Pegasus Books, New York, NY. 2022.

Cityofdouglas.org. City of Douglas, Wyoming official website.

Cowboy State Daily, June 11, 2023.

JOHN
RINGO
JULY 13
1882

The Offbeat Track

The Grave of Outlaw Johnny Ringo

By Kevin Lee Nelson

Outlaws play a large role in the history of the Old West. Perhaps it's not surprising that criminals like Jesse James, Butch Cassidy, and Billy the Kid are just as famous, if not *more* famous, than the heroes of the era, like Wyatt Earp, Kit Carson, Davey Crockett, and Sitting Bull. Outlaws became famous (or notorious) because their audacious exploits captured the imagination of more "civilized" folks out east and across Europe. Their unrestrained and dangerous lifestyle epitomized the lawless nature of the frontier, and their lives were romanticized and celebrated just as gangster John Dillinger was a generation later.

Generally speaking it's more sensible for criminals to keep a low profile and not attract too much attention, but in the Wild West, attention and notoriety was exactly what most of these ruthless men (and some women, like Belle Starr) craved. In the late 1800s, wanted posters depicting one's likeness was like being on the Hollywood Walk of Fame today; the higher the bounty, the more famous they got.

Outlaws and gunslingers often made names for themselves in a variety of ways. Some chose brazen and daring bank and train robberies and became Robin Hood-like folk heroes. Many became common cattle rustlers. Men more prone to violence, became skilled gunfighters -- mercenaries and hit-men for hire willing to gun down anyone for the right price. The worst kind were the ones that weren't skilled or smart enough to succeed in any of these unsavory occupations, at least for long. They took shortcuts to fame (or infamy) by gunning down famous individuals, usually in a cowardly way with no honor, to make a name for themselves. Perhaps one of the most famous of these was the coward Jack McCall, who shot Wild Bill Hickok in the back of the head while he sat at a table playing poker in Deadwood, South Dakota, on August 2nd, 1876. According to the legend, Hickok had a winning hand, Aces over Eights, a hand that has since become known as "Dead Man's Hand."

Johnny Ringo

One outlaw who exhibited all of these traits was John Peters Ringo (May 3, 1850 – July 13, 1882), known as Johnny Ringo. Ringo first got into trouble while in his mid-twenties when he got involved in the Mason County War in Texas from 1875-1876, sometimes called the "Hoodoo War." The "war" was started by a vigilante group of ranchers calling themselves the "vigilance committee." Frustrated with the lack of law and justice in the area, they conducted midnight raids and took the law into their own hands by breaking into jails and lynching suspected cattle rustlers. It was a strange conflict where Texas Rangers found themselves fighting alongside outlaws and cattle thieves against mobs of vigilante ranchers. Texas Ranger Scott Cooley and his friends, including Johnny Ringo, conducted a terror campaign against the rival ranchers. On September 25, 1875, in the war, Ringo, along with a friend named Bill Williams, rode up to the house of rancher James Cheyney seeking revenge. Cheyney had previously led their friend Moses Baird into an ambush and killed him. Cheyney greeted them unarmed and invited them in. While he was washing his face on the porch both Ringo and Williams shot and killed him. Shortly after, Ringo and Scott Cooley were jailed for the murder of Charley Bader, but they were broken out before they saw trial, and later Ringo was acquitted for the crime.

A few years later Johnny Ringo appeared in Cochise County, Arizona Territory, in 1879, but wherever Ringo went trouble soon followed. In December 1879, a drunken Ringo offered Louis Hancock a complimentary drink of whiskey in a Safford, Arizona, saloon. Hancock refused, stating that he preferred beer. Angered by the refusal, Ringo shot the unarmed Hancock, though Hancock survived. Ringo wandered south to Tombstone where he developed a reputation as having a bad temper. It's speculated he may have participated in robberies and killings with a loosely associated group of outlaws, the Cochise County Cowboys.

On January 17, 1882, a hot-headed Ringo and Doc Holliday traded insults and threats and seemed headed for a gunfight. Readers may be familiar with this scene from the blockbuster 1993 film, *Tombstone,* with Michael Biehn playing Ringo and Val Kilmer playing Doc Holliday. Both men were arrested by Tombstone's chief of police, James Flynn, and fined for carrying weapons in town. It may surprise some readers that in many Wild West towns firearms were forbidden within town limits, concealed or otherwise. In the case of Tombstone, guns and long knives were outlawed within town limits in April of 1881 due to frequent violence. However, not everyone chose to obey the new laws. A long-simmering feud between the Cochise County Cowboys gang and the Earp brothers (Wyatt, Morgan, and Virgil), along with Doc Holliday, eventually erupted into the famed Gunfight at the O.K Corral on October 26, 1881 when the gang refused to hand over their guns. The legendary shootout took less than a minute, and when the dust cleared, Billy Clanton and the McLaury brothers were dead, and Virgil and Morgan Earp and Doc Holliday were wounded.

But that wasn't the end of it. Johnny Ringo was suspected by the Earp brothers of ambushing Virgil Earp and crippling him for life, and also the cowardly murder of Morgan Earp, shot in the back while he was shooting pool in a Tombstone saloon. Wyatt, newly appointed as Deputy U.S. Marshal in Cochise County, Doc Holliday, and a federal posse set out to find and kill those they held responsible for ambushing Virgil and Morgan. However, this was complicated by the fact that Cochise County Sheriff Johnny Behan received warrants from a Tucson judge for arrest of the Earps and Holliday. Behan deputized Ringo and 19 other men associated with the Cochise County Cowboys.

Wyatt Earp killed one of Ringo's closest friends, "Curly Bill" Brocius, in a gunfight at Iron Springs. After that Ringo knew his days were numbered. In July of 1882 Ringo had been drinking heavily in Tombstone during the Fourth of July celebrations. He left town a few days later with several bottles of liquor for the ride. Ringo was spotted two days later by deputy Billy Breakenridge near Dial's Ranch in the South Pass of the Dragoon Mountains. He later wrote, "Ringo was very drunk, reeling in the saddle." He encouraged Ringo to follow him back to the Goodrich Ranch, but "he was drunk and stubborn and went on his way. I think this was the last time he was seen alive." Around 3pm on July 13, ranch hands at a nearby ranch heard a shot.

The next day a local laborer from nearby Turkey Creek found Johnny Ringo's body slumped against an oak tree with a bullet wound in his temple. A revolver with one bullet missing was found by his side. He was missing his boots, and instead had strips of cloth wrapping his feet. His horse was found a few miles away, indicating his horse may have gotten away from him. This is where the fate of Johnny Ringo gets murky. Some assumed it was suicide, but others thought that the Earps had finally caught up with Ringo. In fact, in several interviews later in his life, Earp seems to take credit for Ringo's death. Another theory is that Doc Holliday killed him, which is how Ringo's death is portrayed in the movie *Tombstone*. However, the majority of evidence points towards suicide. He was buried right where he died.

The *Tombstone Epitaph* published, "Many friends will mourn him. And many others will take secret delight in learning of his death." Ringo had a reputation for being one of the deadliest gunfighters in the West. Only it wasn't true. There's no proof that Ringo was responsible for any of the killings attributed to him with one exception: that of the murder of James Cheyney. Far from being a skilled gunman, his only verified murder was an unarmed man with a towel over his face.

A few years ago, I drove out to the remote site, about twenty miles northeast of Tombstone, as the crow flies, on the western edge of the Chiricahua Mountains. It's a tricky drive down very rough dirt roads. The grave sits on private land next to Ringo Pond and is now an Arizona Historical Landmark. The land owners graciously allow public access between 8am and 6pm. There are still some oak trees at the site, some old and some fallen. I couldn't help but wonder which tree he was found leaning against. It's a peaceful spot, the kind of spot one might choose if deciding to end one's life. Ringo's grave is marked with a stone marker and a plaque. It might seem strange to commemorate a hot-tempered vigilante and murderer, but Johnny Ringo's important place in the history of the Wild West cannot be argued. Hard and violent times create hard violent people.

Grave site of Johnny Ringo State Historic Landmark

E Turkey Creek Rd, Pearce, AZ 85625.

HISTORIC SITE
JOHN RINGO
THE REMAINS OF THIS NOTED GUNMAN AND OUTLAW LIE HERE. A TEAMSTER TRAVELING FROM WEST TURKEY CREEK FOUND THE BODY SITTING IN THE FORK OF A NEARBY OAK TREE WITH A BULLET HOLE IN THE RIGHT TEMPLE.
A CORONER'S JURY REPORTED THE DEATH TO BE SUICIDE, AND RINGO WAS BURIED ON THE SPOT. THERE WERE OTHERS WHO VIEWED THE BODY AND MAINTAINED THAT THE JULY 13, 1882, DEATH OF RINGO WAS MURDER.
COCHISE COUNTY
ARCHAEOLOGICAL and HISTORICAL SOCIETY
and THE ARIZONA HISTORICAL SOCIETY

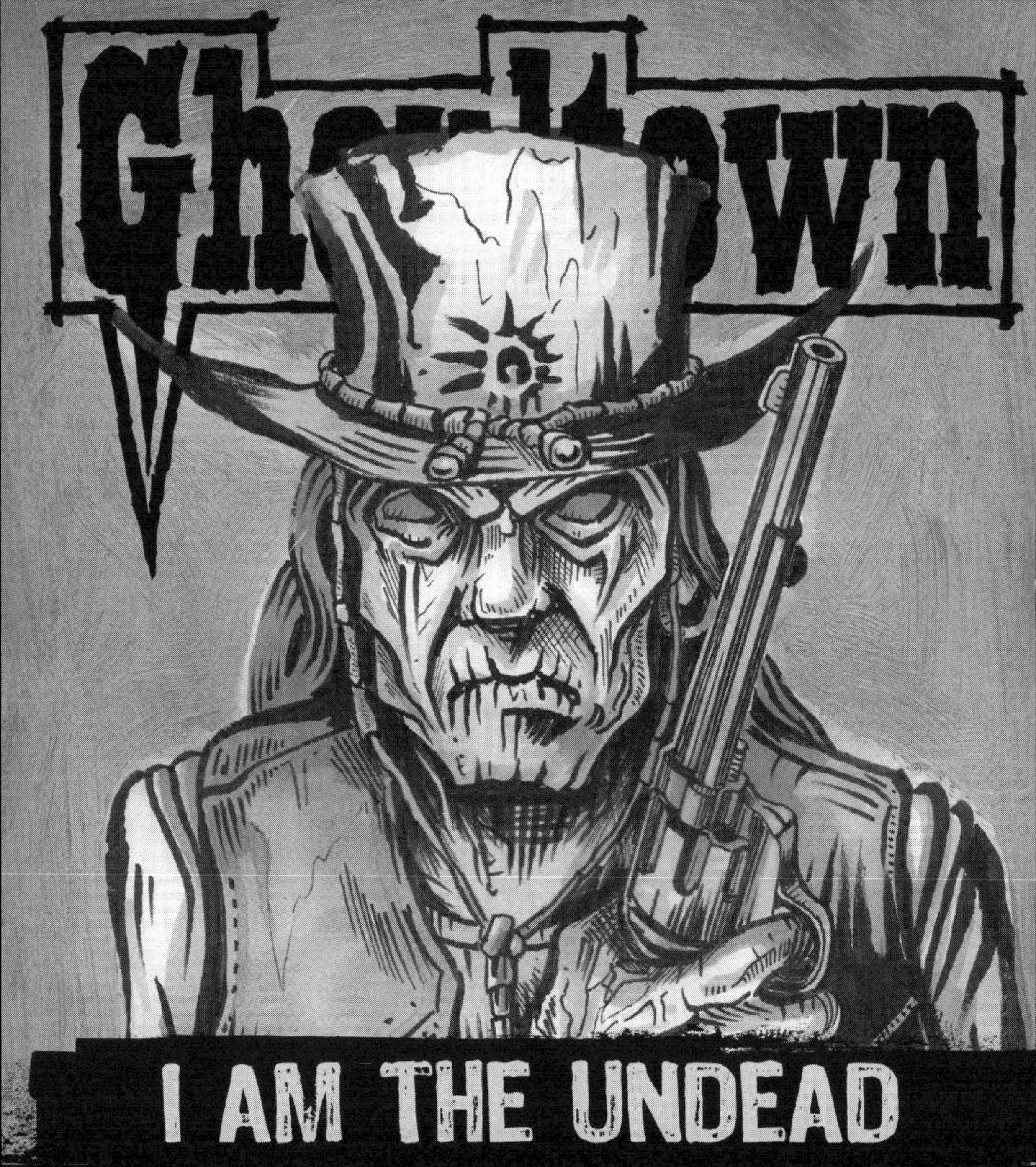
I AM THE UNDEAD

The Digital Campfire

The Weird, Digital West

By Chad Lewis

In 2023, sales of video games exceeded 57 billion dollars as tracked by the Entertainment Software Association. One of the most popular genres in this field is the wild west. Whether it is merely surviving the harsh life of the pioneers or taking hold of an undead gunslinger hell-bent on revenge, the wild west continues to amaze and entertain us.

If you are of a certain age, your first foray into the digital world of the wild west most likely came with the 1971 release of *The Oregon Trail*. This text-based strategy game pitted your wits against all the real-world factors that were out to kill you. If you didn't choose your actions wisely, the game featured a myriad of ways to meet your fate, including snakebites, hunting accidents, disease, starvation, and perhaps the most notable—You have died of dysentery. Although it allowed players to become acquainted with the trials and tribulations of western life, nothing supernatural occurred.

The 1980s saw the release of several wild west games, most notably *Law of the West*. These too lacked any paranormal themes or elements as they mostly consisted of the player being able to take control of a lawless town through the eyes of a sheriff or marshal. It was a strange lack of any supernatural themes mashed with supernatural creatures since the first vampire themed game, *The Count*, was released in 1979. Here the protagonist is sent by the humble villagers of Transylvania to hunt and destroy Count Dracula. Even the smash hit success of 1986's *Castlevania*, in which the player is responsible for killing Dracula, did not open any possible mash up ideas. As one might expect, Dracula is the most prevalent villain in most games, yet the Count doesn't seem to transfer well to the wild west.

The trend of leaving out any aspects of the supernatural in the wild west would change dramatically with the 2005 release of Darkwatch. Players now had the exciting chance to play a first-person shooter where the hero was an outlaw gunfighter who had been turned into a vampire and was being forced to hunt other species of monsters against his will. This introduced the audience to the idea of stepping outside of the norm and approaching play with a darker agenda. Although the game received mixed reviews from critics, there is no doubt it was barreling down the right path towards future popular games.

One of the most popular franchises in gaming history is that of the Red Dead Redemption games. For a lot of people this game might have been their first introduction to one of the most iconic symbols of the wild west---the Jackalope. If you are not familiar with the legend of the Jackalope (check out the Jackalope article in this volume) or if you have ever stopped at a roadside tourist gift shop, then you have probably seen a replica of a Jackalope for sale. Looking like some bizarre cross between a jackrabbit and an antelope, the Jackalope is one of the most widely-known and most iconic examples of the western mythical creatures. If it weren't for its large deer-like antlers, the Jackalope might be easily mistaken for a large rabbit. In the Red Dead Redemption game, the player has the option of hunting down and even skinning Jackalopes.

The Jackalope also makes an appearance in the Guild Wars 2 game, which is a bit weird since the game has more of a Middle-Ages fantasy-type play. However, it should be noted that although the Jackalope is known as a western desert creature, legends of it come from all parts of the United States.

With their Undead Nightmare expansion pack, Red Dead Redemption expanded on the wild west folklore by featuring the hero, wild west gunslinger John Marston, as he desperately searches for a cure for an infectious undead plague that is taking over the world and turning out a never-ending supply of zombies. Similar to vampires, the undead zombies needed to be exterminated before everyone could be considered safe.

Today, wild west games are almost as synonymous with themes of the supernatural and paranormal as they are of tumbleweeds and dusty corrupt frontier towns. Vampires and zombies are by far preferred paranormal monsters of choice in many of these titles, and nowhere is that more evident than with Evil West (2022). This third-person shooter allows the player to control the main character, a six-gun toting, vampire-hunting hero whose mission it is to eradicate the vampire scourge from the planet. To the uninitiated it may seem as though all the wild west/supernatural video games tend to conflate the folklore of zombies and vampires, often making the two practically interchangeable. Yet, if one looks at the creatures from the lens of traditional folklore, it may make more sense. Modern portrayals of vampires have formed them into gorgeous models who freely roam the upper echelon of high society. Although these emotionally sensitive aristocratic super-humans need blood to survive, they have conveniently discovered a never-ending supply of human hosts willing to become their victims in exchange for an eternal life of ecstasy. Yet, vampires were not always cast in such a positive light. In fact, early descriptions of these nightwalkers describe them as hideous mindless ghouls who were hellbent on consuming the blood and flesh of humans. Early vampires did not even possess the ability to communicate and were universally viewed as undead beasts. They reeked of foul, rotting flesh and had rancid breath. Vampires of Eastern Europe were also clad in tattered rags, which were the dirt smeared remnants of their final burial outfit. When you look at vampires from an historical viewpoint, the similarities to video game zombies becomes quite apparent.

It was also in 2023, that the combining of the supernatural and the wild west came to the ultimate mash up with the release of *Blood West.* Not only did it present the theme of being an undead gunslinger steadfast in his mission to rid evil supernatural monsters from the land, the game designers also created a promotional video featuring the band Ghoultown. For those who are unfamiliar with the music of Ghoultown, the band's lead singer is Lyle Blackburn, who is widely known for his books dealing with cryptozoology. Not only that, but the song featured in the video was co-written by David Weatherly (co-author of this book). The game changed its description from a wild west themed game to that of a weird west game.

What will the future bring for folklore and the wild west? I can answer that in one word—Paranormal. I believe that the trend in the next few years will be a more pronounced blending of the genres. When it comes to video games, the designers have only scratched the surface of the plethora of folklore available to them. Yes, a couple of games include the Jackalope, but what about a game that features the roughly 100 other unbelievable creatures the lumberjacks spun wild tall-tales around? As remarkably fun as it might be to obliterate mindless zombies, imagine fighting wild west sea serpents. One only has to think about the movie *Aliens and Cowboys* to see what might be possible for future wild west games. Regardless of where these themes ultimately end up, I am absolutely convinced that folklore will be right beside it.

The Spirited Streets of Tombstone

By David Weatherly

Known as "The Town Too Tough to Die," Tombstone is one of the most well-known towns of the old west. Located in southern Arizona, Tombstone was founded due to the tenacity of a prospector named Ed Schieffelin. According to legend, one day Ed was looking out toward the mountains where present-day Tombstone stands and thought the area looked like a promising place to do some mining. Schieffelin commented on this idea to a soldier who told him the area was controlled by the Apache. "All you'll find in those hills is your tombstone," the soldier told Schieffelin.

The prospector ignored the warning, and in February 1878 he struck a rich vein of silver. Remembering the soldier's comment, Schieffelin staked two claims dubbing one "Tombstone" and the second "Graveyard." Both spots were converted to mines and soon the prospector soon established two more mines dubbed "Lucky Cuss" and the "Toughnut."

A mining camp was established and in short order, a town—named after Ed's first claim—Tombstone.

As silver was pulled out of the mines, Tombstone boomed. By 1881 there were around 8,000 people in the town, and it overflowed with saloons, gambling halls and the largest red-light district in the Southwest.

The town became filled with a wide range of people from miners, merchants and bankers to gamblers, gunslingers, and prostitutes. Along with the sudden influx of people came trouble and Tombstone quickly gained a reputation as one of the most violent towns in the west.

Like many other old west towns, when the mines began to run dry, the town started to lose citizens who left for richer pastures in newer boom towns.

In 1929, the Cochise County seat was moved from Tombstone further south to the bustling copper mining town of Bisbee. But unlike other busted towns, Tombstone survived. Walter Cole, editor and owner of the *Tombstone Epitaph*, dubbed his city “the town too tough to die,” and citizens took it to heart. When the town began to celebrate and promote its wild west connections, things turned around.

The history of the wild west was built into the very fabric of the town, so locals took advantage of what they had to offer. The process of restoring historic sites began and the community started taking advantage of events from the town’s past, especially focusing on the growing interest in the gunfight at the O.K. Corral.

During its heyday, a veritable who’s who of famous western figures strolled down the streets of Tombstone. Wyatt Earp and his brothers Virgil and Morgan, Doc Holiday, Josephine Marcus, Ike Clanton and his cohorts, the list goes on and on. This history and connections to famous figures, coupled with Hollywood blockbuster films like *Tombstone* and *Wyatt Earp*, made the town a tourist mecca drawing in fans of films, the old west, and history in general.

If all of this isn’t enough, there’s another big draw that brings people to Tombstone—ghosts!

Haunted Streets

There's so much ghostly activity in Tombstone that even the streets themselves are said to be haunted. The apparitions of ghostly cowboys have been seen in town, sometimes strolling casually as if merely going about their business unaware that time has passed them by. These phantoms may be residual haunts, recordings if you will, impressed on a town once charged with energy and excitement where emotions ran high.

The ghost of Marshal Fred White is also said to haunt the streets. White was the first marshal of Tombstone and had a lot of dealings with the Clantons and their cohorts. The rugged cowboys respected White, however, so he had few problems with them and was able to keep them from getting too out of hand.

In the early morning hours of October 28, 1880, Curly Bill Brocius and some other men were carousing in the streets shooting their guns off in a wild spree. White went out to disarm the men before any citizens were killed, but he was shot in the groin by a stray bullet fired by Brocius. Doctors initially thought White would survive, but he never recovered, and he died two days after the shooting.

White was shot in an empty lot where the Bird Cage Theatre was later built. His ghost has been seen in the street in front of the Bird Cage, the last place he was up and walking around.

Another phantom seen on the streets is a tall man in a long black frock coat. The figure is typically seen starting to cross the street, but he never makes it to the other side. This odd fact has led some to believe that it's the spirit of Virgil Earp who was ambushed one evening as he walked out of the Oriental Saloon. Although he wasn't killed in the incident, the shooting did result in Earp losing the use of his left arm, leaving him crippled for the rest of his life. Perhaps the ghost is merely a residual haunting of the infamous moment that changed a man's life for good.

Billy Clanton, who was killed during the fight at the O.K. Corral, is also believed to haunt the streets of the town. And some people have claimed to see his ghost around the area where he was shot down.

Given that many buildings in old west towns were quickly-built wooden structures, fires were a grave concern. In southwestern towns like Tombstone, the dry conditions and wind-swept landscape created a deadly combination, and fires could spread rapidly with flames leaping from one building to another in rapid succession.

Tombstone suffered two major fires in a short period of time. The first was in June 1881, the second in May 1882. Both fires destroyed a large portion of the town's business district. When the fires broke out, the saloons, brothels and gambling dens were packed with people drinking and carousing. More than forty people are known to have perished as a result of the two fires.

It's believed that the spirits of some of these fire victims still wander the streets of Tombstone today. Witnesses have reported seeing ghosts with terrible burns and others have caught the smell of smoke filling the air even when there's no visible fire in sight.

One woman told me that she and her sister were walking around Tombstone one evening in 2007 when they had a startling encounter.

"We saw two cowboys walking toward us. We thought maybe they were part of the gunfight show, but when they got closer, we saw they looked like they had burns all over their faces. My sister and I looked at each other in shock, both of us asking 'do you see them.' When we turned back there was nothing there."

O.K. Corral

The mere mention of Tombstone brings to mind its most famous spot, the O.K. Corral—location of the most famous gunfight of the old west.

The battle was a result of rising tensions between two factions in Tombstone—on one side were the Earp brothers and their friend Doc Holliday, and on the other the cowboys including the Clantons, McLaurys and their cohorts.

The battle took place on October 26, 1881, when Marshal Virgil Earp set out to disarm some cowboys who were carrying weapons in Tombstone—a violation of a city ordinance. The cowboys refused to surrender their guns so Earp, his brothers, and Doc Holliday faced the men down. The gunfight was quick and fierce with some thirty shots being fired in thirty seconds. When the smoke cleared, three men were dead—Billy Clanton, and brothers Frank and Tom McLaury—all cowboys.

The gun battle has been depicted in numerous films, documentaries and

television shows over the years and it has been studied extensively by western historians who have examined every movement of the men involved. The gunfight is an integral part of the legends of both Wyatt Earp and Doc Holliday.

Today, the O.K. Corral is the town's most popular tourist spot. It's also said to be haunted—a fact that is somewhat curious considering that the gunfight did not actually occur at the O.K. Corral. The O.K. Corral fronted Allen Street but had a rear entrance on Fremont Street. Horse stalls lined the back entrance of the corral. The gun battle itself occurred in a narrow lot on the side of C.S Fly's photography studio on Fremont Street—a spot six doors west of the O.K. Corral's rear entrance.

Despite the distance and the battle not taking place right at the corral, there are numerous reports of ghosts lurking around the building today. Some people claim they've seen the ghost of some of the gunfight's participants, guns drawn and ready to shoot it out to the death. Perhaps this is a residual impression of the iconic confrontation or perhaps it's just a projection from those enraptured by the town's history. Many of these reports come from people in front of the corral on Allen Street, rather than at the actual gunfight location.

Witnesses who see apparitions around the O.K. Corral describe phantoms in classic cowboy attire. Other witnesses have reported odd cold spots around the site, and some have claimed to hear disembodied voices and phantom gunshots.

One death that did take place right at the corral was that of Justice Jim Burnett. Burnett was feuding with a man named William Greene. On June 24, 1897, one of Greene's daughters died when a dam was exploded, sending water rushing through the river on Greene's property. Young Ella Greene and a friend, Katie Corcoran, drowned in the high water and Greene was devastated by the loss. When he learned that his nemesis Jim Burnett had ordered his workers to dynamite the dam, Greene went on the hunt for Burnett and found him by pure chance on July 1st. Burnett was sitting in the front office at the O.K. Corral conducting some business. The men began to argue and when Burnett rose, Greene thought the man was going for his gun. Greene fired three shots at Burnett at close range and the man staggered away, going through the doors and out onto Allen Street. With blood dripping from his wounds, Burnett fell in front of Haffords Saloon next to the O.K. Corral. By some accounts, Greene shot the man one more time to ensure that he was dead.

Some people believe that Burnett's spirit still hovers in the street where he met his bloody end. Witnesses have reported seeing a shadow figure that moves from the entrance of the O.K. Corral and into the street where it collapses to the ground and disappears. There are other claims that Burnett's apparition shows up both inside the front of the O.K. Corral and on the street outside.

Today, you can tour the O.K. Corral, see historic items and catch a reenactment of the gunfight. The site is located at 308 E. Allen Street.

Big Nose Kate's Saloon

In September 1880, Tombstone's Grand Hotel opened. Said to be one of the finest hotels for miles around, the Grand was a high-end spot with thick carpets, ornate hand-carved furnishings, and beautiful chandeliers. The hotel had a kitchen with hot and cold running water and there were sixteen bedrooms decorated with lavish wallpaper and upper scale fixtures. The hotel opened with an invitation-only ball, and for a time it was the talk of the town. Among the famous figures who stayed at the Grand were Wyatt Earp, Virgil Earp, and Doc Holliday. Some of the Clantons also stayed at the hotel, and the night before the gunfight at the O.K. Corral, Frank and Tom McLaury and Ike Clanton were all registered guests.

Sadly, the Grand had a short run—it caught fire and burned down on May 25, 1882, less than two years after it opened. Little survived the inferno. On the ground level, the hotel's arches and floor joists made it, but most of the rest was reduced to ashes and debris with much of it collapsing down into the basement.

Now at the spot where the Grand once stood is one of Tombstone's most well-known saloons—Big Nose Kate's.

The saloon is named after Mary Katherine Horony, aka Big Nose Kate. Kate is best known as the frequent companion of gunfighter Doc Holliday. Despite the saloon's name, Kate never owned a business at the location, but history has given her name recognition.

The Grand Hotel's original bar survived the fire, and it's a center point of the saloon. Kate's is on the main level where the hotel was, and the basement level of the hotel became a gift shop for the saloon. A lot of paranormal activity has been reported at the saloon, and one of the hotspots of strange occurrenc-

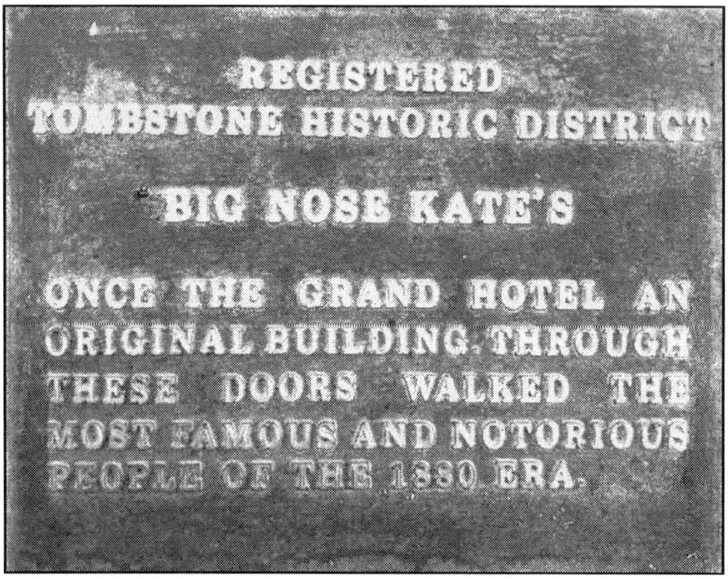

es is the basement which is also home to the saloon's most well-known spirit—"The Swamper." According to legend, the Swamper guards a horde of silver that he hid somewhere on the premises. He's been seen all over the bar, but he's most often associated with the basement.

Reportedly, the Swamper was a man who worked at the Grand Hotel when it was in business. The man worked as the hotel's janitor and maintenance man and did other odd jobs. The man was said to be a good worker and honest employee. As part of his pay, he was given a room to use at the hotel. Of course, the regular rooms were for paying guests, so the man was given a space in a dark corner of the hotel's basement. Apparently, the fellow wasn't really bothered by the arrangement, in fact, he took advantage of it by doing some tunneling. It seems that the basement of the Grand Hotel wasn't very far from some of the numerous mine shafts that ran under Tombstone. With patience and some effort, the Swamper made his way to a rich vein of silver and started pulling out the valuable metal. It's believed that the man collected a horde of silver that still lies hidden somewhere in what is now Big Nose Kate's Saloon.

It's commonly believed that the Swamper lurks in the saloon in ghostly form, still trying to hold on to his stash of silver. Various incidents of mischief are blamed on the Swamper, including objects that get mysteriously moved about or knocked over. The Swamper is also blamed for items that go missing altogether.

A popular story that has circulated for some time reports that a group of people explored the Swamper's tunnel and discovered that it still led all the way to the mine shafts of the historic Toughnut Mine. When the group turned and went back to the basement of Kate's they heard a creepy moaning sound along with heavy footsteps. The sounds were coming from the stairs leading up from the basement to the bar area of the saloon. Of course, this was unsettling since whoever, or whatever, was making the sounds wasn't visible! A quick investigation of the premises confirmed that the saloon was empty and that all the doors were locked. Some thought that the ghostly sounds were made by the Swamper who was upset at the prospect of his hidden silver cache being discovered.

Additional paranormal activity at Big Nose Kate's includes phantom footsteps, odd noises and cold spots. Cameras have also been known to malfunction or to produce shots that are hazy and blurry.

Disembodied voices have also been heard in the saloon, usually talking in quiet conversation. People have also reported hearing a phantom singing in the

saloon. Some people have claimed to see silverware fly off their tables of its own accord as if swatted by some invisible hand. Another man recalled reaching for his beer that was on the bar in front of him, only to watch as it slid out of his reach. This happened a total of three times with each of his attempts to grab the glass leading to the drink sliding farther and farther away. He finally nabbed the beer glass on his fourth try. The man was careful to emphasize that it was his first drink of the evening so there were no questions regarding his perception or awareness. Perhaps a phantom cowpoke was thirsty! It is notable that some witnesses have reported seeing the ghost of a cowboy standing at the bar. No one's sure exactly who the ghostly cowboy is or why he's haunting Kate's.

Big Nose Kate's bills itself as "The Best Cowboy Bar in the West" and is located at 417 E. Allen Street.

Ironically, Big Nose Kate's ghost isn't even reported at the saloon that bears her name. Her spirit does, however, supposedly linger at another classic Tombstone establishment—The Crystal Palace.

The Crystal Palace Saloon

It should come as no surprise that the ghost of Big Nose Kate is said to haunt the Crystal Palace. During the period that Kate was in Tombstone with Doc Holliday, the saloon was one of her favorite spots in town. In fact, Kate lived at the Crystal Palace for a time.

Paranormal activity at the saloon includes lights turning off and on of their own accord, objects that vanish only to reappear in another location, and disembodied voices.

The bathrooms at the Crystal Palace are also said to be haunted. People report the bathroom doors opening and closing, toilets flushing on their own and the faucets turning off and on of their own accord. Witnesses have also reported seeing a man entering the bathroom who never comes back out. When an inspection of the room is done, no one is found inside—and there's not another way out.

Some witnesses have also claimed to see the ghost of cowboys in the saloon, both walking around at the entrance and standing at the bar.

The Crystal Palace is at 436 East Allen Street.

The Bird Cage Theatre

After the O.K. Corral, the Bird Cage Theatre is probably the next most famous spot in Tombstone. The theatre opened in 1881 and from its opening day until 1883 it remained in operation 24 hours a day. In short order it became the go to place in Tombstone for everything from live entertainment to gambling, booze and of course, prostitutes. The Bird Cage's reputation led to the *New York Times* dubbing it "the wildest, wickedest night spot between Basin Street and the Barbary Coast."

The theatre's name was derived from a series of small cribs that hung from the ceiling. During the heyday of the Bird Cage, the cribs held painted ladies dressed as feathered birds.

Twenty-six recorded deaths took place in the Bird Cage. Evidence of the frequent shootings that happened in the theatre remains today in the form of 140 bullet holes inside the building.

By many accounts, the building is full of spirits ranging from the ghost of

The Original
BIRD CAGE
THEATRE
of Tombstone

cowboys to the phantoms of prostitutes who worked at the site. Many people call the Bird Cage the most haunted spot in Tombstone and the reported activity seems to run a wide gamut. Reports include phantom noises, including the sound of cards shuffling, the clink of poker chips, disembodied laughing and singing, and the clinking of glasses. Some of the ghosts purportedly become rowdy and boisterous at times.

There are numerous reports of apparitions wearing clothing from the 1800s being seen in the theatre. One of the phantoms most frequently reported at the Bird Cage is the ghost of a male stagehand. Clad in black striped pants and a visor, he's often seen holding a clipboard and strolling across the stage as if he's surveying show preparations.

A woman I spoke with in Tombstone in 2014 swore that she'd seen the ghost of a cowboy sitting at a poker table in the theatre. The phantom casually tossed a chip onto the table, then looked up at the witness before fading away.

While there are countless modern reports of ghosts in the theatre, it seems that paranormal activity has been taking place in the building for a long time. In 1921, after a school was built across the street from the Bird Cage, students started reporting the sound of music and laughter ringing out from the theatre. This would have been normal when the business was opened, but by that time, the Bird Cage was shut, and the building was abandoned.

The building had several owners over the years. The theatre shut down in 1889 and for a time, the Bird Cage was badly deteriorating. Fortunately, it was rescued and today it operates as a museum filled with relics of the town's wild west history. The original grand piano is still in place, along with gambling tables, the hand painted stage and the famous cages that once held soiled doves (prostitutes).

Visit the Bird Cage Theatre at 535 East Allen Street.

Schieffelin Hall

Built by Al Schieffelin, brother of Tombstone founder Ed Schieffelin, the hall on Fremont Street was built to bring culture to Tombstone, something that the town's upstanding citizens thought was desperately needed.

The hall was envisioned as a classy alternative to the wild and rowdy Bird Cage Theatre. It opened in June 1881 and was the largest building in Tombstone at the time. It was also the largest adobe building in the Southwest.

Author David Weatherly (center) as Wyatt Earp on stage at Schieffelin Hall

Schieffelin Hall was a grand success and was popular with Tombstone's citizens who came to watch plays, operas, lectures, grand balls and even boxing matches. Performers came in from as far away as New York to appear in productions put on at the location.

When the mines began to play out, attendance at the hall suffered and by the early 1900s the hall was being used to show moving pictures as Hollywood began to take over from live entertainment. After this, the hall was used for a time as a Masonic Lodge, but with Tombstone's boom times over, the hall ended up abandoned.

The hall was eventually fully restored, and in modern times it is used once again for live performances. Aside from actors and singers, it seems that the hall also plays host to a number of phantoms. The distinct sound of a man in boots walking in the hall has been reported by a number of witnesses. His spurs are heard clanking but to date, no one has seen the apparition responsible for the phantom footsteps.

Far stranger than ghostly footsteps are the reports of what sound like chains being dragged around. One man I spoke with at the hall told me that while he knew it sounded ridiculous and cartoonish, he was sure the phantom sound he heard was that of a heavy chain being moved across the floor.

People have also reported strange things on the stage at Schieffelin Hall including disembodied whispers, cold spots, and the feeling of being touched by someone who isn't there.

Schieffelin Hall is at 402 E. Fremont Street.

Boot Hill

Boot Hill, or Boothill, is a term used for burial grounds primarily in the old west. The term alludes to the idea that many cowboys and gunfighters "died with their boots on," meaning essentially that they died in some violent manner.

Some would say you can't have a genuine old west town without a boot hill, and Tombstone certainly checks the box. Primarily used between 1878-1884, the Arizona town's version of Boot Hill was originally named the Tombstone Cemetery. The burial site has more than 250 graves of people who died in the town including a number of famous figures: Marshal Fred White, who was killed by Curly Bill Brocius, and three men killed during the Gunfight at the O.K. Corral—Billy Clanton and brothers Tom and Frank McLaury.

When a new graveyard was established in 1885, many respectable citizens moved their family members out of the old site and reinterred them in the newer cemetery so they wouldn't be buried near outlaws and scoundrels.

There was little to no upkeep on the cemetery grounds for a long period. Many of the wooden markers faded and rotted, others were stolen by souvenir hunters. In 1923 a writer named Frederick Bechdolt started a movement to preserve and rename the site. The site was cleaned up in the 1920s, but it wasn't until the 1940s that preservation efforts finally took hold. The city began to restore and preserve the graveyard and the site was renamed Boothill Graveyard. Sadly, only a small portion of the original site was saved, and the burial records were never located.

Boothill has become one of Tombstone's most popular tourist stops and over the years, many visitors have reported odd occurrences at the old graveyard. Anomalous lights have been seen floating around the graves, people have heard disembodied voices and strange sounds on the property, and there have also been reports of apparitions at the site and some people have captured strange figures in photographs.

Boothill is located at 408 N. Highway 80 and is open daily.

I've spent a lot of time in Tombstone and the spots covered here are but a small fraction of the ghost stories to be found in the town. Wyatt Earp's love, Josephine Sarah Marcus, once reportedly said that "Tombstone had a man for breakfast every morning." Whether that's true or not, there's no doubt that there were many deaths and events in Tombstone that have left a lasting impression on the town.

As one of the most iconic towns of the wild west, the town is a must visit for those interested in western history or the paranormal.

Resources and Works Consulted:

Hawley, Joshua. Tombstone's Most Haunted. Tombstone Paranormal, Tombstone, AZ, 2009.

Tombstone Restoration Commission. Tombstone's Historic Locations.

Traywick, Ben. The Chronicle of Tombstone. Red Marie's Bookstore, Tombstone, AZ, 1990.

Traywick, Ben, and National Tombstone Epitaph. This is Tombstone: The Town Too Tough To Die! Red Marie's Bookstore, Tombstone, AZ, 1984.

The Lady in Red of the Mizpah Hotel

By Kevin Lee Nelson

The History of the Mizpah Hotel

Hotels played a crucial part in the history of the Old West. Pioneers, prospectors, cowboys, and gunslingers all needed places to stay as they passed through towns. Often they were the only place one could get a decent bath other than a cold dip in a creek. Hotels thrived in boomtowns by offering lodging, whiskey, gambling, and prostitution to entice the rough men seeking to carve out a life on the frontier. Many were a symbol of civilization and refinement in an otherwise hard and still untamed landscape. Most are long gone now; lost to fire, economic busts, and the wrecking ball of "progress," but a few have managed to survive after over a century. One of these is the Mizpah Hotel in Tonopah, Nevada, out in the high-desert about midway between Las Vegas and Reno.

The Mizpah Hotel was a bit of a latecomer in the history of the West. The oldest part of the building is the saloon, built in 1901 when the Wild West was becoming a bit more tamed. Seven years later a five-story 56-room hotel, designed by Reno architect George Holesworth, was added at a cost of $200,000. It was considered extremely lavish for the time and was constructed of solid granite walls, leaded glass windows, solid oak furniture, brass chandeliers, steam heat, and included one of Nevada's first electric elevators. At five stories it was the tallest building in Nevada for 25 years. A 1917 advertisement in the *Tonopah Daily Bonanza* for the Mizpah Hotel boasts, "Modern Hotel where every reasonable tariff prevails — hot and cold water running in each room."

The same page includes an ad for the hotel's bar that reads, "The Mizpah Bar is stocked with the choicest drinkables and smokables — a gentleman's resort." Known as "The Jewel of the Desert," the Mizpah Hotel was the center of Nye County social and economic activities and a gathering point for the political elite of Nevada for half a century.

The Mizpah Hotel (1905)

The hotel got its name from a local legend. Tonopah's founder, a prospector named Jim Butler, had a donkey named "Mizpah." According to the legend Bulter's donkey wandered off during the night. When he finally found Mizpah he picked up a rock to throw at the donkey out of frustration only to discover a large vein of pure silver running though the stone. He had discovered the second-richest silver strike in Nevada history, which later became Mizpah Mine. Of course, like many legends, there are always different versions of the story. Others say Butler found the silver because he married a local Paiute woman named Belle, and her family guided Butler to the area long known by indigenous peoples for its minerals. Mizpah, the hotel's distinctly Jewish name, means "watchtower" in Hebrew and comes from a prayer in the Old Testament asking God to keep watch over travels (Genesis 31:49).

Nevada legalized gambling in the 1940s, and the Mizpah didn't waste any time converting its lobby into a casino, including a roulette wheel, craps table, blackjack, and 80 slot machines. During its century of operation the hotel changed hands many times until it eventually closed its doors in 1999. It remained shuttered for 12 years until the grand old hotel was meticulously restored to its former glory in 2011. Today it's on the National Registry of Historic Places.

Over the years many notables frequented the Mizpah Hotel. World heavyweight boxer Jack Demspsey tended the bar and worked as a bouncer at the Mizpah. Reclusive billionaire Howard Hughes married actress Jean Peters at the hotel. It's said that Wild West legend and gunfighter Wyatt Earp ran off claim-jumpers in near-by Goldfield and allegedly often relaxed at the Mizpah. Some say he even ran the bar for a while during the area's mining heyday. It's an interesting story, but it's unlikely, as Earp left Tonopah just before the hotel was built. Even so, today the saloon in the hotel is named after Wyatt Earp. Key Pitman, Nevada senator from 1913 to 1940, was a frequent guest at the Mizpah. According to legend he died at the Mizpah on the eve of the 1940 election. His supporters kept his body on ice in a hotel bathtub until the election was over and his successor could be appointed. The hotel's Pitman Cafe is named after the senator. Many other celebrities and dignitaries have stayed at the Mizpah over the years. But arguably their most famous guest is one that never left, The Lady in Red.

Who was the Lady in Red?

While gentlemen conducted business in the hotel's saloon, restaurant, and lobby, others conducted their business upstairs. Like many Wild West hotels, the Mizpah had other business activities going on behind the scenes. According to the Central Nevada Museum, the Mizpah Hotel was never a brothel, at least officially. While still trying to keep an upscale and genteel appearance, it seemingly turned a blind eye to what was going on upstairs as long as it wasn't too overt.

Prostitution was common in Tonopah in the early part of the century, which had an extensive red light district. Up to three-hundred dance girls and another three-hundred "hurdy-gurdy" girls worked in the town's red light district. Prostitution mostly fell into three types of establishments: brothels, cribs, and independent upscale "ladies of the evening." Brothels were establishments that offered prostitution as their main source of income and were managed by a madame who collected payment for "services" outside of food and gambling. Cribs were a step down from brothels and were controlled by pimps. They

Portrait of the Lady in Red hanging in the Mizpah Hotel Lobby

were sparsely furnished rooms, often not more than simple shacks with a bed, pot-bellied stove for heat, and a water bucket. It was a miserable life for "working girls". On a busy night they could see up to 80 men an evening. In Tonopah, they were not allowed to work outside the red light district or allowed in any of the uptown bars.

On the high end, and far more rare, were the independent contractors: the "ladies of the evening," what we would call expensive escorts today. Only a handful of women were fortunate enough to have this much control. They often had permanent lodgings at upscale hotels and were often cultured, dressed in fine clothes, and didn't stand out among the other affluent guests. Their clientele was mostly wealthy men who required discreetness and were willing to pay top dollar for exceptional beauty.

According to the legend, the Mizpah Hotel had a year-round resident who went by the call name "Rose." She worked from a lavish 5th floor suite, discretely away from most of the action below. Other versions of the legend say she was a secret mistress or "kept woman" with a rich patron who paid for all her needs. A number of sources indicate "Rose" may have been Evelyn Mae Johnson, born in Baltimore in 1879, but this has never been confirmed. Unfortunately for Rose, if the stories are correct, she was stabbed and strangled by a jealous lover and died in the hall just outside her room, #502. Most reports say this occurred on January 2nd, 1914, though *The Mizpah Review*, the hotel's newsletter, said that Rose arrived in Tonopah sometime in the 1920s.

Other versions speculate that she was a married woman whose husband discovered her with another man after he returned to the room unexpectedly after missing his train. In a fit of rage he began strangling her and dragged her out of the room (room 502) where he stabbed her to death in the hall outside the room between 502 and 504. None of the tales say what happened to the other man. According to hotel manager Tracy McCormick if you pull up the carpet in that spot you can still see blood stains on the wood flooring.

Strangely, there are no official reports of a murder from that time. Murders certainly happened in Tonopah and frequently made headlines, yet there are no reports of a woman being murdered at the Tonopah Hotel, or the murder of a woman at all in town. The *Tonopah Daily Bonanza* mentions nothing about a murder of a woman in the weeks following the date of the alleged murder. Some have theorized that the murderer, possibly the wealthy patron or husband with powerful connections, depending on which version is to be believed, had the funds and means to cover it up. A body was never discovered. Granted, it would have been easy to dispose of a body in a remote desert mining town full of mine shafts. The sudden disappearance of a wife would require some explaining, but the disappearance of a prostitute, no matter how high-end, would generally go unnoticed.

The Haunting Begins

But some say that Rose never left. After her murder, guests reported seeing an apparition on the 5th floor. It's unknown when the sightings first began, but we do know that encounters with the apparition have been reported for a long time. Eventually she became known as "The Lady in Red." There is a large portrait of a beautiful dark-haired woman in a fancy red dress in the hotel lobby that is supposed to be a representation of the Lady in Red. However, the Lady in Red didn't get her name from the color of her dress. I spoke with a hotel staff member about the legend, and she told me the story has been sanitized quite a bit over the years to make it less scary and gruesome. You see, she isn't called the Lady in Red because of the color of her dress — she's called the Lady in Red because the front of her pale dress is stained red with blood and gore.

In the paranormal field so-called "Women in White" or "White Lady" type hauntings are a well-known phenomena around the world. According to legends and folklore, Women in White apparitions are usually associated with themes of loss, usually an accidental death, murder, suicide, betrayal, or an unrequited love. A Lady in Red or Red Lady is a variation or sub-set of this type of female ghost but is more specifically attributed to the spirit of a jilted lover, a women killed in a fit of passion, or women of vanity. The Mizpah's Lady in Red falls into this category. There are also Blue Ladies, Green Ladies, Lavender Ladies, and Black Ladies, the latter considered to be the most malevolent.

White Ladies (and all the sub-set color variants) are often considered "residual hauntings," as they tend to haunt a particular place, usually the location of a tragedy, replaying their final moments over and over like a looped recording. Reports of interactions are rare, though some claim their purpose is to reveal a dark secret, like who murdered them, where something important is hidden, or where someone is buried. Stories of Women in Black often represent omens of death or involve a curse of some sort. Other famous White Ladies (and other hues) around the country include:

- The Lady of White Rock Lake (Dallas, TX)
- The White Lady of Avenel (Bedford, VA)
- The White Lady of Whopsy (Altoona, PA)
- The White Witch (Fremont, CA)
- Resurrection Mary (Chicago, IL)
- The Lavender Lady of Lemp Mansion (St. Louis, MO)
- The Lavender Lady of Moonville Tunnel (Moonville, OH)
- The Blue Lady of Palmetto Dunes (Hilton Head Island, SC)
- The Blue Lady of Moss Beach Distillery (Moss Beach, CA)
- The Green Lady Of Wahiawa (Wahiawa, HI)
- The Woman in Black (Roanoke, VA)
- The Lady in Black of Fort Warren (Boston, MA)

- Huggin' Molly (Abbeville, AL)
- The Lady in Red of the Drake Hotel (Chicago, IL)
- The Red Lady of Huntingdon College (Montgomery, AL)
- The Bloody Bride (Stevens Point, WI) She is also covered in blood like the Lady in Red at the Mizpah.

These are just some examples of legends from around the nation, and there are many, many more.

5th Floor outside Room 502

The Mizpah's Lady in Red is most often seen on the 5th floor near where she died, though others have claimed to see her in the elevator. Men report hearing a female voice whisper sweet nothings in their ears, only to turn and find no one there. Over the years many guests have reported finding a pearl beneath their pillow — supposedly from The Lady in Red's pearl necklace that spilled to the floor during the violent struggle that ended in her death.

Eventually her large suite was split into three rooms, rooms 502, 503, and 504. 504 is officially the "Lady in Red Room" furnished with scarlet curtains and period furniture. Unlike many hotels that attempt to downplay or avoid discussing their ghostly occurrences, the Mizpah has embraced the legend. They know that eerie tales are an attraction for many people, especially in the last twenty years, as ghost tourism has become a major economic boon for haunted locations. In fact, in 2018 the Mizpah was ranked the #1 Haunted Hotel in America by USA Today 10 Best Readers' Choice Awards. Staff at the Mizpah say if you happen to capture anomalous phenomena in a photograph they will give you 50% off your stay. The legend has become so popular that the hotel offers ghost tour packages for guests.

While at the Mizpah I brought up the legend with a middle-aged housekeeper on the 5th floor to see if she had any personal experiences with The Lady in Red. She was very happy to talk about it and share her stories. As it turned out, she had a number of sightings during the time she's worked there. After talking for a while about different sightings she'd had of the Lady in Red, I asked her if he had managed to take any photographs or video. It turned out she did. She pulled out her phone and shared a video she had taken showing a mysterious ball of light floating down the hallway and making a right turn towards room 502. But what really impressed me was she also had an image she took of the hall outside room 502. In the picture I could clearly see a ghostly figure of a woman standing just around the corner with a large dark stain down the front of her pale dress. It was exactly in the spot where it's claimed that Rose was stabbed to death. It was an amazing photo -- possibly one of the best potential spirit photographs I've ever seen. It did not appear staged at all. I'm not going to lie — the hair stood up on the back of my neck. After all, I was standing just a few feet from where the entity was standing in the photograph.

Inside Room 502

Other Spirits of the Mizpah Hotel and Tonopah

The Lady in Red is certainly the most famous spirit at the Mizpah, but many visitors to the 116-year-old hotel claim the place is crawling with ghosts. A mysterious soldier allegedly haunts the 3rd and 4th floor. The 3rd floor is also known to be haunted by a pair of children that are often heard giggling and running up and down the hallway late at night. It's said they like to play pranks on guests by opening and closing doors. Guests will call down to the front desk to complain about the noise only to find out that there are no children staying at the hotel.

The story of running ghost children seems to be a an extremely common story at haunted hotels. I've encountered this story, or slight variations of it, at roughly 75% of the allegedly haunted hotels across the nation, and I've stayed at over a hundred of them, though I have yet to hear the giggling and the pitter patter of small phantom feet myself. So either it's a story that's been shared a lot and attributed to a number of places, or small children are highly prone to haunt hotels.

Photo of alleged apparition

If that wasn't enough, the Mizpah staff claims the basement is haunted by two bank robbers. Part of the current hotel was originally constructed as a bank, and the bank's vault was located in the basement. It's where a lot of the area's gold and silver ore was kept for safekeeping. The walls and ceiling were constructed of 3-foot-thick concrete; almost impenetrable, but not from underneath. Three robbers tunneled under the vault and broke in through the vault's floor. However, after they got in, one of the robbers got greedy and wanted all the gold and silver for himself, so he shot the other two, left their bodies in the vault, and took off with the loot. He was never captured and the gold and silver was never recovered. Now staff members (and some guests on hotel ghost tours) claim to hear mysterious whispering, coughing, and knocking from around the area of the vault.

Besides the Mizpah Hotel there are plenty of other ghosts in the area, including another haunted establishment just down the road from the Mizpah. I would be remiss to write an article about Tonopah ghosts and not mention the infamous Clown Motel, arguably one of the creepiest motels in America. The entire motel is clown-themed (yes, every room). Someone actually thought that would be a good business model. It's probably not a place you want to stay if you have caulrophobia (irrational fear of clowns). I spoke with Marlena who co-owns the hotel with her husband, and she filled me in on the motel's history.

The Clown Motel was built in 1984 by Larry David in honor of his late father, Clarence, who loved clowns and circuses. He wanted his father to be happy in the afterlife, so he built the motel right next to a pioneer graveyard figuring it would be easier to visit by the souls of the dead. Read that again -- The Clown Motel sits right next to a graveyard! According to guests, Larry succeeded, as many claim it's extremely haunted.

Marlena said the whole place is haunted, but especially room 216. She gave me the key to 216 and let me go check it out. I took four steps into the room and my phone went from 40% charge to zero. I went out to my car and got a backup battery with a full charge, but I was only able to take a few shots with my phone camera inside the room before it went dead too.

People often describe seeing black shapes moving throughout the motel and report hearing mysterious carnival music. Guests frequently find their items moved and placed in unusual locations, not where they left them. Marlena believes the restless spirits of the dead move between the graveyard and the motel. The graveyard looks like it's right out of a Clinton Eastwood Western. Most of the people buried in the graveyard met violent or early deaths. A casual survey of the wooden grave markers proved this to be true: murder, suicide, tuberculosis, mining accidents, etc.

The Clown Motel is easily one of the strangest places I've ever seen. The juxtaposition between the creepy clown themed motel and the old graveyard is a masterstroke of eeriness. In contrast, the Mizpah Hotel is a classy time capsule of a bygone era that, while certainly spooky, is not wall-to-wall bizarre like the Clown Motel. Visitors to Tonopah have the option to pick an appropriate level of terror that is right for them. Overall Tonopah is a fascinating and historic town that still feels authentic, offering a glimpse into what the Wild West was like. Perhaps that's because souls from its boomtown heyday might still linger about and walk its streets at night.

Resources and Works Consulted:

McCracken, Robert. *A History of Tonopah, Nevada*. 1990.

Oberding, Janice. *Haunted Nevada: Ghosts and Strange Phenomena of the Silver State*. 2013.

Ridgeway, Virgina., and Janice Oberding. *Mizpah Hotel: History, Happenings and Hauntings*. 2019.

Tonopah Daily Bonanza. September 14th, 1917.

The Mizpah Hotel. https://themizpahhotel.com/.

USA Today. https://10best.usatoday.com/awards/travel/best-haunted-hotel-2018/

The Clown Motel

Welcome to
Deadwood
Gold Rush 1876

The Dead Are Alive in Deadwood

By Chad Lewis

Deadwood. The name alone conjures images of old wild west gunslingers, disreputable gamblers, gold prospectors, boisterous fighters, and all manner of unscrupulous characters wandering down tumbleweed infested dirt roads. The place is such an exemplary example of the authentic wild west that instead of going building by building surveying the historical significance, the U.S. Department of the Interior simply decided to designate the entire town as a National Historic Landmark.

The discovery of gold in the Black Hills of South Dakota in 1874 set in motion a mass influx of those looking to strike it rich. Practically overnight, gold rush fever put Deadwood on the map. The town was soon bustling with miners, shop keepers, gamblers, horse thieves, prostitutes, and all sorts of other outlaws looking to ply their trade in the newly formed outpost of the west. As news of the new wild unruly town spread, Deadwood attracted the daring, the bold, the thrill-seeking, and the adventurous—people whose names would quickly become synonymous with the wild west. Surrounded by gorgeous, rugged countryside, and even more rugged people, the town rapidly developed a reputation as a place where anything goes, and as you will soon see, Deadwood more than lived up to its reputation.

Today, Deadwood is a thriving tourist town providing visitors a chance to step back in history and experience the buildings, people, and culture that once dominated this lawless town. Similar to the 1800s, a lot of people visit Deadwood for the gambling—as modern-day casinos have made it more civilized, and mostly eliminated the chances of you losing your life over a hand of poker. Others take full advantage of the outstanding scenery and wildlife that encompasses the Black Hills region. However, it is the history of the area that is the undisputed main attraction of Deadwood, as curious travelers revel in the chance to explore what the wild west was like in the 1800s. Perhaps it is this intense longing to experience the past that keeps the dead alive in Deadwood, as ghostly apparitions and haunted places continue to draw the bold and adventurous to town. The list of infamous spirits lurking around Deadwood is like a who's who of wild west characters. So, let's take a tour of Deadwood and get acquainted with some of its most visible dead citizens.

Upon arriving in Deadwood your first point of business is to follow in the footsteps of those who have been venturing to the town for the last 150 years---and find yourself some suitable lodging. Luckily, Deadwood is full of lodging options---everything from luxury suites at one of the upscale casinos to more rustic mom and pop motels on the outskirts of town. My advice is for you to lean toward history and book a room at one of the two most historical (and haunted) locations in town---The Bullock Hotel or the Silverado Franklin Hotel. Let's start with the Bullock.

The Historic Bullock Hotel

Seth Bullock played an instrumental role in the early formation and growth of Deadwood. In 1884, Seth Bullock met a young Theodore Roosevelt and the two became fast friends, and Roosevelt would eventually appoint Bullock as the first Forest Supervisor of the Black Hills. Bullock possessed a true entrepreneurial spirit. In 1895, Bullock had the ambitious plan to open a three-story sixty-room hotel that would cost him nearly forty-thousand dollars to construct, and take nearly two years to complete. He would name the place the Bullock Hotel. In 1896, the Grand Hotel opened to great excitement. Business was so good that in 1900, an addition to the hotel was added. Becoming a U.S. Marshall in 1905, Bullock looked to bring law and order to the rowdy outlaw town. Bullock was known far and wide as an imposing man with an ice-cold stare that gained the respect of even the most hardened criminals. Those who knew him best stated that he could outstare an angry cobra and send a rampaging elephant to its retreat.

In 1919, Bullock succumbed to cancer and passed away in room 211 of his hotel. His body was buried in Mt. Moriah cemetery alongside other notable Deadwood characters. If you want to stare down his grave, you will find it on top of the large hill in the cemetery, However, if you don't want to make the trek out to the boneyard, you can simply visit the Historic Bullock Hotel where you might just have the opportunity to stare him down face-to-face because out of all the Black Hills places that Bullock loved dearly, none compared to his own beloved hotel. Bullock adored the place so much that even after death, it remains his favorite place to linger—and it seems his spirit is not alone as numerous other ghosts have also seemingly checked in forever.

Seth Bullock

In room 211, the room where Bullock met his death, guests frequently report seeing his spirit meandering through the room. One couple told me that while staying in Bullock's room they went out to explore the history of the town. When they returned to their room, it was as though a tornado had blown through; everything was strewn about and messy, even though nothing was missing and no cause of the disturbance could be found. If you are not lucky enough to stay in Seth's room, don't fret, his spirit does plenty of wandering through the entire hotel.

Those who are unaware of the hotel's haunted reputation often find themselves getting a puzzling lesson in the paranormal. One man was staying at the Bullock and had no idea of the haunting activity that has made the hotel famous. He was extremely puzzled when he saw the ghost of a tall, stern-looking man walking down the hallway near his room. The witness reported that the ghost just disappeared right before his eyes. After seeing a photo of Seth Bullock, the man was convinced that he had seen the ghost of Seth near his room. It should be noted that Seth's ghost is one of the most encountered ghosts of the hotel. Many of the witnesses' report noticing the unmistakable stare that made

Seth so feared and respected while he was alive. The ghost of Seth Bullock also seems to appear when employees are taking a long break or working at a slow pace. Many believe that even from the grave, Seth is trying to keep a watchful eye over his employees.

My absolute favorite story involving Seth's ghost came from a couple who were staying in room 306 with their seven-year-old grandson. Like most kids of that age, the lure of the hotel's vending machine proved too much, and the young boy begged for a treat. Armed with a couple of dollars, the kid set off for some tasty treats. After making his selection, the young boy got turned around and started aimlessly wandering the hallways in search of his room number. After some time had passed, the boy's grandfather began to worry and opened up the door to go search for the boy. Much to the grandfather's surprise, his grandson was standing right in the doorway. The young kid explained that he had gotten extremely lost and fortunately a nice man finally helped him find his way back to the room. The next day, while the family was checking out of the hotel, the young boy pointed to a picture of Seth that was hanging on the lobby wall and exclaimed, "That is the nice man who helped me find my room."

Seth's ghost is not the only spirit lingering in the hotel, as many others have reported seeing the apparition of a young girl lingering in the hotel. Her spirit is mostly seen in the basement of the hotel which is the location where young children were kept during the typhoid fever and smallpox outbreak in Deadwood. It is also the spot where many of those same children met their demise.

Some of the most fascinating experiences at the hotel come by the way of mysterious sounds that plague the building. Both staff and guests have reported hearing the eerie sounds of phantom footsteps in the hallways of the hotel. Those brave enough to peek out of their rooms never find the cause of these footsteps. Several perplexed guests have reported hearing the lonesome sound of a woman weeping through the night. Sometimes this eerie wailing is accompanied by a crying child, but no source is ever located.

Whoever is haunting the hotel, and this is obvious—they like listening to country music. Staff and guests that tune the hotel radios to a rock station report that the radios will inexplicably flip back to a county music station. One evening a woman staying in room 313 marched down to the front desk in the middle of the night with the hotel's alarm clock in hand. She reported that she had been unable to sleep due to the alarm's big light, so she decided to unplug it. However, at approximately 2:30am the alarm went off by blasting country music into the room. The woman was so scared she refused to keep the haunted

alarm in her room. Another guest of room 313 raced down to the front desk in her pajamas claiming that she had just awoken from her sleep and spotted an apparition of a weird man in a cowboy hat hovering at the foot of her bed. The woman was so distraught over her ghostly sighting that staff members had to pack up her belongings because she refused to go back to her room.

During the popular Days of '76 Festival, a cowboy was enjoying an afternoon nap in his room when some unruly person kept rapping on his door. Unable to sleep, the irritated cowboy positioned himself next to the door—waiting for the prankster to strike again. Sure enough, a few moments later, the incessant knocking began and the cowboy cracked open his door and noticed an unfamiliar cowboy standing in the hallway. As he fully swung open the door to confront the joker, the other man was nowhere to be found. Just then, someone, or something shoved the man from behind with such force that he stumbled into the hallway and his room door was slammed shut behind him.

Those who spend time in the hotel's casino often catch a scent of roses or

lilacs wafting through the hotel. Strangely, the spectral smells occur more frequently in the winter months when natural flowers are not in bloom.

In the basement of the hotel sits Seth's Cellar Restaurant. For whatever reason, this area is home to numerous puzzling events. Several staff members told me that while they were working, the hotel piano would mysteriously begin playing old ragtime music on its own. It is believed that the ghostly pianist is upset that the restaurant was moved from its original location inside the hotel. Plates and glasses from the restaurant are often seen being moved by some unseen force. I spoke with one such witness who, along with four of his friends, witnessed a plate unexpectedly fly from the shelf and come crashing down to the floor. A staff member quickly cleaned up the mess, grumbling that the ghost did this type of thing all the time. Both guests and staff report that the barstools in Bully's Bar will be moved around or toppled over by some unseen hand. Others report that the chairs will rearrange themselves as though someone or something was not pleased with their placement.

Apparently, some of the spirits have a mischievous side as guests frequently report lights in their rooms being turned on and off on their own. Housekeepers told me that while cleaning up guests' rooms, they would often find that their carts had been moved and hidden.

One of the most common apparitions spotted throughout the hotel is that of a tall imposing man who is often seen walking through the halls before disappearing into thin air. Some guests are not lucky (or unlucky enough) to actually see the spectral man, but they often hear him. On numerous occasions guests have heard a deep voice of a man call out to them, although no one else was around. The identity of this mysterious apparition is unknown. Perhaps, it is Seth Bullock and the witnesses are unaware of what he looked like, or perhaps just another forgotten character from Deadwood's past.

If you find yourself scared out of the Bullock Hotel, don't worry, you can always check into the historic Silverado Franklin Hotel.

The Silverado Franklin Hotel

While this hotel does not possess the sheer number of odd occurrences that the Bullock does, it has more than enough weird legends to keep its occupants on high alert. Opening in 1903, the opulent hotel was the talk of the region. In the early days, the hotel hosted many distinguished guests like Theodore Roosevelt, Babe Ruth, John Wayne, and Buffalo Bill Cody. Unfortunately, financial hardship settled in on the hotel, and the once glorious building was converted into residential apartments. When gambling was legalized in 1989, the building was once again turned back into a hotel. Many contend that all the renovations and structural changes have stirred up numerous spirits who keep a watchful eye over the goings on.

One of the most frequently spotted spirits is that of an elegant-looking man strolling through the place as though he owns it. Impeccably dressed as though he just stepped out of the early 1900s, the ghostly figure often watches over the staff as they work, almost as though he is keeping tabs on the quality of their work. Due to the spirit's interest in making sure the place is running smoothly, it is thought that the ghost is that of the hotel's founder, Harris Franklin. Guests are not spared from his critical watchful eye either as many have reported getting the sense that someone is always watching them while they stay at the hotel.

Whenever I have visited the hotel, staff members have told me of all sorts of little daily things that strike them as odd. While cleaning up the guests' rooms, workers will hear heavy footsteps stomping down the hallway, but when they take a quick glance, no one is found. Workers often catch a fleeting image out of the corner of their eye, appearing as though someone is walking down the hallway, but when they turn to get a better look, the hallway is completely empty.

Now that you have your lodging squared away, it is time for you to immerse yourself in all the weird and wild history that Deadwood has to offer. It is time to wake the dead, and take a leisurely stroll out to Deadwood's most infamous graveyard....

Mount Moriah Cemetery

Mount Moriah is the most popular cemetery in the region for good reason--it is filled with larger-than-life characters. Wild Bill Hickok, Calamity Jane, and Seth Bullock are just a few of the iconic wild west figures that are laid to rest in the cemetery. However, it appears that it is the unsung souls of the cemetery that are causing a lot of the haunted activity.

Perched on top of a hill on the edge of town above Deadwood Gulch rests the sprawling Mount Moriah Cemetery. Burials here date back to the 1870s. It is believed that over 350 infants and children who died from outbreaks of diphtheria and scarlet fever are buried inside the cemetery. In addition, a large portion of the over 3,500 people buried here died from natural disasters, freak accidents, or were killed in the lawless days of the town. The Deadwood Cemetery Association provides a long list of various causes of death from those who lost their lives. As one might imagine in a wild west town, the list proclaiming the cause of death reads like an old western dime novel:

- Bad Whiskey
- Dropsy of the Heart
- God Knows
- Killed by Indians
- Hanged by Vigilantes
- Opium
- Hobnail Liver

Every year, thousands of tourists visit the historic graveyard looking to pay their respects to the wild west characters buried inside. The most common report from unsuspecting guests is being overcome with the sense that someone is watching them as they move from gravesite to gravesite. No matter how many times people look over their shoulder or glance around, they can't shake the feeling that they are not alone.

In the early days of Deadwood, a large portion of Black Hills mine workers were Chinese. The backbreaking work was extremely dangerous and deadly, as most bosses believed it was more economical to simply replace dead workers than to implement costly safety precautions. Knowing the treacherous conditions of their employment, the immigrant workers had secured labor contracts that guaranteed that within 10 years of their death, their bodies would be disinterred and shipped back to China for a proper burial. The widely-held belief among the workers was that if their bodies did not receive a proper burial in Chinese soil, their souls would be damned to wander for all of time. Instead of fulfilling their promises, most of the employers unceremoniously dumped the dead men in unmarked graves and forgot all about them. Knowing this, it should then come as no surprise that today's visitors to the cemetery report seeing the spirits of the Chinese workers wandering through the cemetery at night---forever prohibited from an eternal rest. These out-of-place spirits leave witnesses with an odd sense of remorse and dread.

In 2005, I spoke with two employees of the cemetery who would often experience odd things while at work. While preparing to close up the cemetery, it was the girls' responsibility to walk about the grounds to ensure that no visitors were still mulling about inside the gates. While passing by gravestones the girls would routinely spot shadowy figures moving throughout the cemetery. No cause for this was ever found. Another employee informed me that one of her closing duties was to go through the cemetery and close all the gates. On several occasions she would properly close a gate and then spin around quickly to see that someone or something had re-opened the gate she had just secured.

While closing up in the gift shop, employees told me that they would often hear the sounds of people engaged in lively conversation coming from inside the cemetery. Convinced that some visitors had not exited the graveyard, the employees would walk back there to escort the guests to the exit, only to find that no one was there. The disembodied voices were heard so frequently that employees began brushing it off as just another anomaly of the cemetery.

Others will hear the tell-tale sounds of children laughing, playing, and having a wonderful time. Yet, when staff goes to investigate the commotion, there is no sign of any children—alive or dead. Of course, most attribute these ghostly sounds as coming from all the children buried there who met an untimely death. Several employees that I talked with were so spooked by all the happenings inside the cemetery that they refused to work alone.

Once you are done paying your respect to the dead, it is time to let off a little steam and enjoy the entertainment side of Deadwood.

Wild Bill Bar

Arguably the most infamous of all Deadwood residents was the notorious Wild Bill Hickok. The well-known and feared gunslinger arrived in Deadwood in 1876. However, even Bill's reputation as someone you did not want to tangle with could not spare him from this treacherous town. Not long after arriving in the rough and tumble town, Hickok found himself in an intense game of poker at Saloon #10. While engaged in the hand, Jack McCall came up behind Hickok and shot him dead. Apparently, when he was killed Hickok was holding a pair of aces and eights in his hand, thus forever cursing that poker hand as "dead man's hand."

Wild Bill Hickok

Unfortunately, the original Saloon #10 building was burned to the ground. In the late 1800s, the building was rebuilt and continued to operate as a gambling house and brothel. The ladies of the night operated on the second floor. In 1980, when prostitution was finally outlawed in Deadwood (Yes, 1980!) the upstairs of the building sat closed, but maybe not empty, as many would report hearing the scandalous sounds of the building's previous past. First floor employees could also hear the footsteps of someone walking back and forth on the second floor, although it was completely void of any living people. The second floor is also the spot where visitors and staff have seen the image of a young child moving about before disappearing into thin air. Some contend the young spirit is the illegitimate child of one of the brothel's patrons.

Today the location where Wild Bill met his end is home to the Wild Bill Bar where you can check out the spot where the murder took place. Some believe that the spirit of Wild Bill continues to haunt the cursed spot where he died.

The above-mentioned locations are just a few of the nearly endless places in Deadwood where the past continues to mix with the present. Just as the entire town has been designated as a National Historic Landmark, there are so many haunted legends in town that it may just be easier to say the entire place is haunted.

Resources and Works Consulted:

Deadwood Cemetery Association. Deadwood, South Dakota.

Lewis, Chad & Fisk, Terry. *The South Dakota Road Guide to Haunted Locations*. Unexplained Publishing. 2006.

Tommyknockers

By David Weatherly

In the 1800s, the mining industry began to grow and expand rapidly in the United States. The expansion meant that experienced miners were needed, and they soon came from Europe. A large portion of the miners came from Cornwall and Wales and in the 1820s, they took up work in the coal mines of the east. These men knew their trade well, and in short order, their numbers spread across the country moving from the coal mines to the gold and silver mines opening in the west.

Territories that later became states like Nevada, Colorado and California were some of the hotspots for those hoping to strike it rich, or at least, to have steady work.

Mining was a risky business with plenty of hazards. Dangerous gases could be an invisible killer spreading toxic fumes and poisoning the air. Tunnel collapses were a constant threat. Fires in mine shafts were common and perhaps the thing that miners feared the most—after all the idea of being burned to death underground would chill anyone to the bone.

With the unique working conditions and numerous dangers, it should come as no surprise that the men who worked in mines developed a range of superstitions related to their jobs. For instance, it was considered bad luck for a woman to enter a mine. If a man's clothes fell off the hook, it meant he was going to fall into a hole. If rats or mice were seen running out of a mine, a cave-in was imminent…the list goes on. But along with their superstitions and folklore, the European miners also brought their stories of underground dwellers. Known variously as "knockers," or "knackers," these little men became commonly referred to as "Tommyknockers" in the United States.

Tommyknockers dwell deep in the earth. They are described as small, gnome-like men about two feet in height with large heads and wrinkled skin. They are typically dressed in mining attire. By some accounts, they are bearded with white whiskers while other stories say they are clean shaven.

Tommyknockers are both helpful and troublesome, depending in large part on how they are being treated by miners in the area where they live.

The name itself is derived from the little people's propensity to "knock" in the mines. This tapping noise was often seen as a message that danger was present—Tommyknockers are said to knock in warning when a mine collapse was imminent. Wise miners hearing the sound would abandon the mine, lest they be trapped inside under piles of rubble with no escape. Miners who escaped tunnel collapses often credited the Tommyknockers for their salvation.

Some miners claimed that the tapping sounds made by the little people was code and they interpreted it in varying ways. A "tap, tap" sound may signify a spot to dig, whereas a triple tapping sound meant there was nothing at the spot. In other words, the sounds were an elaborate method of communication similar to morse code.

Some miners even reported a strange knocking on their knees or elbows that they believed were the Tommyknockers giving them warnings of impending danger.

Knocking is one thing, but in some cases, the little people were said to take even more direct action if a miner found himself in trouble.

In *Tales, Trails and Tommyknockers*, author Myriam Ackley reports an incident where one of the little men saved a miner's life. Ackley writes:

"Once a miner stood on a rock in the middle of a deep pool of water. Suddenly, invisible hands pushed him hard from behind. Kerplunk! He splashed into the water. As he swam away, a huge boulder fell right on the spot where he'd been standing."

Tommyknocker legends were originally tied very strongly to the Cornish who comprised a large portion of mining immigrants. Western historian Marshall Trimble notes that "over a quarter of a million Cornish, or some 20% of their population, immigrated to America between 1860 and 1900" (*True West*, June 2023).

The Cornish were regarded as the best hard rock miners in the world. The miners were a close-knit group. The miners soon became known as "Cousin Jacks." According to folklore, this term arose from mine owners asking their Cornish employees if they had any relatives who might want to work in the mine. A typical reply was "Well, me cousin Jack in Cornwall would come 'if ye could pay 'is boat ride.'" (Jack was purportedly a very common name in Cornwall at the time.)

Plenty of "Cousin Jacks" made their way to America to work in the mines, but they would typically refuse to even enter until they had assurance from the higher ups that the Tommyknockers were already in the mines.

According to some legends, Tommyknockers slipped into the luggage of men from Cornwall who were headed to America to work the mines. Once in the states, the crafty little men quickly made their way into mines around the country, claiming a whole new territory for themselves and their kin.

There's plenty of lore and superstitions associated with Tommyknockers. It was considered bad luck to shout at them, curse them, or even talk about them in negative or derogatory terms. To do so would bring their wrath.

Good will with the Tommyknockers was created by the sharing of food and general consideration and courtesy toward them. Some miners left out a portion of their lunch for the little men every day; others brought specific treats to give them. Small cakes or pasties were some of the common offerings. Such treats might be left out somewhere for the knockers to take at will, or tossed into the mine itself as a way of giving it to the little men.

It's also said that Tommyknockers could help miners locate riches, leading them to valuable veins of gold or silver.

If a miner was roused between the hours of midnight and two a.m. by the sound of the little people tapping, it was a sign of good fortune. If the miner followed the knocking sound, the Tommyknockers would lead him to a rich vein of ore. If the miner lost his way while following the trail, he could tap on the walls and the little people would respond by tapping back and continuing to guide him until he reached the proper spot.

According to an article by Marshall Trimble in True West, a Cornish gentleman named Gassy Thompson reaped the benefits of listening to the Tommyknockers. Thompson was a lone miner out west—well—he was sort of alone. Reportedly, he had two companions, a dog named Digby and an unnamed rattlesnake. Thompson had supposedly found the rattler when it was an orphaned baby and made a pet out of it. The miner kept the snake around and in turn the snake controlled the rat population at Thompson's home.

Gassy purportedly trained the snake to spot gold nuggets that he himself had missed. Whenever the rattlesnake would find a nugget, it would wrap itself around the gold and start to rattle until Gassy came and retrieved the ore. Gassy claimed that snake even found a pocket of gold worth around three thousand dollars.

The veracity of such outrageous tales is of course highly questionable, but it seems that Gassy really was finding a lot of gold. According to some, the miner's real secret wasn't a trained rattlesnake at all but his ability to listen to the Tommyknockers. Trimble writes:

"During the hot summers Gassy would search for gold in the cool confines of the abandoned gold mines. There he learned to communicate with the Tommyknockers, and they would tell him where to look for gold; then Digby would do the manual labor.

"There were skeptics who were prone to doubt Gassy's method of finding gold, but one thing is certain—according to the local merchants, Gassy always found more rich pockets of gold than all the other desert rats combined."

Such beliefs led to many miners taking great care to be respectful towards the Tommyknockers and to give them offerings.

Those who chose the opposite path—that of joking about the little people

or scorning them—found a world of trouble waiting for them. The trickster-like nature of the Tommyknockers could cause them to commit random acts of mischief. Typical examples of such behavior included stealing a miner's tools or food. Sometimes, the tools would reappear in unusual places. As for the food, well, usually it was never seen again! If the offense or insult was more serious, the consequences might be as well. The offending miner might find himself pelted by stones from an unseen source, or find himself lost in a mine shaft.

Some traditions state that the Tommyknockers could be downright sinister if provoked and that they could bring about misery, injury and even death to those who crossed them in some way.

On occasion, the little people could be so troublesome that mines were forced to close. Cursed mines were also sometimes attributed to the presence of Tommyknockers. There were mixed feelings as to why this was the case. Some believed the little men were simply chasing miners away because the whole area was unsafe and prone to cave-ins while some believed the little men just wanted to be left alone and have the mine for themselves.

Cornish miners placed so much importance on the Tommyknockers that they would refuse to enter a mine unless it was clear that the little men were on duty and present in the shafts. Mine owners frequently stated that the "Tommyknockers were on duty" in order to reassure European miners who showed up to work the site.

Since the Cornish viewed the Tommyknockers as a species of little people, they were careful to help look out for them when they could. A great story comes from Dave Tabler at the Appalachian History website who notes that in 1956 the owners of a large mine in California decided to shut down their operation and seal the mine entrance. A group of miners circulated a petition demanding that the owners open the entrance and let the Tommyknockers out so they could move on to other mines. The owners complied with the workers' request.

The workers were descendants of Cornish miners—fourth, fifth and sixth generation miners.

According to some traditions, Tommyknockers aren't little people at all but are the ghosts of miners who perished while working underground. Stuck in a ghostly form, these spirits linger in the afterlife and warn the living of dangerous conditions and threats. This version of the Tommyknockers developed later and is not as prevalent as the belief that the knockers are a race of gnome or dwarf-like beings.

An odd variation of the Tommyknockers as having a ghost origin says that they are the spirits of Jewish miners who were enslaved by the Romans and forced to work in mines. This variable of the legend claims that Tommyknockers were allegedly never heard on Saturdays or during Jewish religious festivals. This variation turns up in Robert Hunt's 1908 book *Popular Romances of the West of England: The Drolls, Traditions, and Superstitions of Old Cornwall.* The author writes:

"The Buccas or Knockers are sprites of the mines and correspond to the Kobals of the German mines, the Duergars and the Trolls. They are said to be the souls of the Jews who formerly worked the tin-mines of Cornwall."

Hunt adds that the spirits were "not allowed to rest because of their wicked practices as tinners."

In an essay in *Western Folklore,* Ronald James oddly notes an odd combination of different pieces of Tommyknocker lore, making them little creatures who are apparently Jewish…or maybe Christian. James writes:

"The Knockers were diminutive and elf-like and observed the Jewish Sabbath and several Christian holidays by abstaining from work. They punished curiosity and greed and rewarded people who treated them kindly. The Knockers could be mischievous and were easily offended. They did not like whistling or being watched. Their knocking could lead miners to wealth or warn them of danger."

It's interesting to note that at some point, people began reporting that Tommyknockers could take up residence in homes located near mines. Here, too, they continued using knocking as a way to communicate with humans. In this case, a superstition says if a strange knocking sound is heard in the house, it meant that someone in the family was going to die.

These fascinating folkloric traditions have held strong for decades, and despite the fact that the process of mining has changed significantly, Tommyknocker tales still arise in modern times and there are still reports of encounters with little people near mines.

Folklorist Caroline Bancroft writes in her essay "Folklore of the Central City District, Colorado" about the little men:

"The belief about 'Tommy-knockers,' the dwarflike creatures who inhabit the mines and who cause any unexplained phenomenon occurring underground, was still active in the camp in the '30s. One foreman told me that in 1931 he had two miners throw up their jobs in the Chain-O-Mines workings of Quartz Mill because 'the Tommy-knockers are keeping a cow in there.' He went in himself and heard a sound exactly like a cow mooing—a very weird occurrence deep in the bowels of the earth, which gave even him something of a turn. Upon investigation, it proved to be water dropping and sliding across a sheet of tin in such a way as to swirl and reverberate into the eerie sound. But the foreman could not get the miners to go back and see for themselves."

In her research, Bancroft only found negative impressions of the Tommyknockers. She notes: "In the district they are considered troublemakers in their least malevolent form, carrying away tools, causing missed holes, and the like. But generally, if they are believed in at all, they are feared as dangerously sinister."

In 2011 I received an email from a woman who told me that her family had a story about her grandfather's encounter with what he believed was a Tommyknocker in the 1940s. At the time, the man was working at a small mine with two other men. The trio was sitting outside not far from the mine entrance. They were preparing to get back to work after a break when they heard a sound behind them. Turning around, the miners saw a little man making off with some of their tools. The miners jumped up and chased the man a short distance, but he quickly vanished from view. They found their tools on the ground behind some bushes and as they were standing there puzzling over the incident, they heard a noise from the mine shaft—there had been a collapse. All three men retired from mining after the incident and they firmly believed that the little man—a Tommyknocker—had saved them from being trapped, or worse, killed in the mine that day.

It's notable that in this instance, one of the miners had a habit of leaving bits of food out for the Tommyknockers. Perhaps his sharing of food ultimately paid off.

Responding to the Tommyknockers article on the Legends of America website, California resident Allan MacLaren writes:

"My father grew up in a mining camp [in] Confidence, California. His father worked at the Confidence mine. Father's stories of those times included the Tommyknockers. Your recital is right on. My father said his mother would bake a saffron cake for his father to take with him. When the miners (the cousin Jacks) finished their day, they always left some saffron cake for the Tommyknockers. To not do so was very bad luck.

MacLaren notes that he grew up in Ohio and that his grandmother had baked a small saffron cake when she visited, so the tradition, at least part of it, continued in the family.

In 2015 I met an old timer in Virginia City, Nevada, whose family had a long association with mining in the region. The man's grandfather had been a miner, and so had several generations of men in the family prior to that. He was well familiar with the Tommyknocker legend himself and said that he'd first heard of the little men when he was a young boy and had listened to stories about them told by his grandfather.

"They're little men in mining gear," John told me. "They'll take care of you if you're kind to them, but if you cross 'em then look out, they'll run you off with all kinds of troubles."

John told me that he'd seen one of the Tommyknockers himself when he was a young man. He said he was about twelve years old at the time. He was out with his grandfather one day and the older man had to make a stop at a mining site to speak with someone. John's grandfather told him to stay by the pickup truck until he returned, so the boy sat on the tailgate of the truck eating a sandwich while he waited. John recalled:

"It was a dry, dusty day. I was eating that sandwich, just looking around when I saw something sticking its head out from behind some rocks close by. It was this little guy, looked like a dwarf to me. I don't know why but for some reason I thought he looked hungry, and I thought he was eyeing my sandwich. I took the other half and held it out toward him. He licked his lips, but I could tell he was afraid to come out from behind the rocks."

John says he walked slowly over to the rocks where the little man was hiding. As he approached, the figure sunk back behind the boulders and out of sight. John stood there for a moment hoping the little man would pop back up. When he didn't, John put the sandwich down on top of a big rock and then walked back over to the truck.

"I climbed back up on the tailgate and looked back over but the sandwich was already gone."

John finished the rest of his half of the sandwich, then pulled out two cookies that he had in his bag. He walked over to the rock again and placed one of the cookies in the spot where he'd left the sandwich half. As he started walking back to the truck, he reconsidered, turned around, and left the second cookie on the rock as well.

"That little guy just looked so hungry to me that I wanted to give him both of my cookies. I figured I'd get some dinner when I got home but I didn't know if this fellow had anything else to eat."

Just as with the sandwich, by the time John got back to the truck, the cook-

ies were gone. The boy continued to sit on the tailgate waiting for his grandfather. He kept glancing back over toward the rock hoping to see the dwarf again, but there was no sign of him. John thought perhaps the little man had left since all the food was now gone, but the boy had another surprise coming.

"I'd say about five minutes or so after the cookies were gone, I looked over there at that rock and saw something shiny. I went over to it again and I found a shiny silver coin had been left in the spot where I had put the sandwich and cookies."

John specified that the little man he saw was around two-two and a half foot tall. He had a green hat, and he wore a brown jacket. He did not have a beard, but John says he had wrinkles around his eyes and his features were somewhat exaggerated, which, to John's eye, gave him a rather jolly appearance.

As for the coin that was left, the young man went and retrieved it only to find that it was an old silver coin from England. John's grandfather was stunned when he saw the coin, and when the boy told the older man about the encounter, his grandfather told him he'd been fortunate and that he had received a gift from a Tommyknocker.

"He told me not to tell anybody else about it and to keep the coin safe and not spend it. I carried that coin with me for years and I always believed that it brought me good luck."

John was in his eighties when I met him, and he had passed the coin on to his adult son a couple of years prior to our discussion. John added:

"I got no reason to lie or keep the story secret anymore. There's a lot of things out in this world that most people don't know about. I know there's another race of people, little people that live here 'cause I met one when I was young. Seems that they stay mostly hidden. Can't say as I blame them."

Hidden they may be, but the rich lore of the Tommyknockers continues to fascinate people even today and they have shown up in various forms of media in the modern era. A popular craft beer company in Idaho Springs, in Clear Creek County, Colorado, is named the Tommyknocker Brewery. The brewery was named after the legendary little people, and the business even uses an image of one of the wee folk as its logo.

Tommyknockers became known to a whole new audience when horror author Stephen King published a novel titled "The Tommyknockers." Included in the book was a short rhyme that King had purportedly learned in his childhood:

"Late last night and the night before,

"Tommyknockers, Tommyknockers, knocking at the door.

"I want to go out, don't know if I can,

"'Cause I'm so afraid of the Tommyknocker man."

The exact origin of the rhyme isn't clear as there don't seem to be any records to indicate exactly where the verse came from. King grew up on the East Coast and lived in various places during his youth and exactly where he heard it or who he learned it from has not been made clear either.

Given the origin of the Tommyknockers, it would seem that the rhyme would most likely have come from Cornwall; however, this doesn't seem to be the case. I spoke with my friend Mark Anthony Wyatt who's well versed in Cornish lore—having lived much of his life there—and he was unfamiliar with it. Enquiries to other associates proved equally unsuccessful in determining the true origin of the verse although some thought it might have been an old nursery rhyme that had different words. In short, if the rhyme is of Cornish or European origin, no one seems to recall ever hearing it! If it did indeed come over with early miners and their families, you would think there would be an earlier record to indicate that's where it's from. Whatever the case, it stuck in many people's minds. Strangely, beyond the name, King's Tommyknockers have nothing in common with the little ones from folklore. King's book is a science fiction romp set in Maine that involves a crashed alien spaceship.

Beyond advertising and entertainment, one wonders if the Tommyknockers still wander the tunnels of America's mines. The modern era of mining is a world apart from the traditional trade that helped build the country. Massive machines have taken the place of jobs that were once done by many men.

Whereas hazardous ropes and buckets powered by mules and human hands used to be employed to lower people into the depths of the earth, there are now mechanical elevators with countless safety precautions. Ore is no longer extracted by handheld picks and tools but by high tech implements. Perhaps, some might think, the Tommyknockers are no longer needed.

In 2014 I spoke to Carl, a young man in Nevada who shared a story about an abandoned mine he'd come across. He and two friends had gone into the desert to do some exploring when they came across a boarded up mine entrance. One of his friends was eager to pry the planks off and venture inside, but Carl adamantly refused, telling his friends how dangerous such shafts could be. As the three stood there arguing, they heard a distinct tapping sound coming from the mine entrance.

"It sounded like a metal pickaxe striking stone," Carl told me. The three young men stood there listening to the eerie sound coming from the old mine. It was a chilling feeling to think that someone—or something—was in the mine, and they elected to turn and leave the place alone.

Many such abandoned mines dot the landscape of the west. While they may seem intriguing, they are, nonetheless, quite dangerous to enter. Many of these sites are purportedly haunted, but it might not be the phantoms of the dead lurking inside, but rather some small little figure who knocks away in warning whenever anyone ventures too close.

Resources and Works Consulted:

Ackley, Myriam. Tales, Trails and Tommyknockers: Stories from Colorado's Past. Bower House, Denver, CO, 2018.

Bancroft, Caroline. Folklore of the Central City District, Colorado. California Folklore Quarterly, Vol 4, No. 4, Western Folklore Society.

Hunt, Robert. Popular Romances of the West of England; or, The Drolls, Traditions, and Superstitions of Old Cornwall. London, Chatto & Windus, 1908.

James, Ronald M. "Knockers, Knackers, and Ghosts: Immigrant Folklore in the Western Mines." Western Folklore, Vol 51, No. 2, April 1992.

Legends of America website, Tommyknockers.

Tabler, Dave. Tommy Knockers & Mine Ghosts. AppalachianHistory.net.

Trimble, Marshall. "Cornish Miners and Tommyknockers," True West magazine, June 2023.

Jarbidge: Land of the Cannibal Giant of Northern Nevada

By Kevin Lee Nelson

One of the most isolated and remote towns in the lower 48 states is a small unincorporated community called Jarbidge in northern Nevada. The nearest town of any size is roughly three hours away. There are only three ways to get down into the canyon where Jarbidge is located. One from the Elko direction requires a 100-mile trek over deeply rutted dirt roads. Without a vehicle with high clearance, like a Jeep, you're likely not going to make it. The next option is a 50-mile dirt road from Mountain City Highway, but snow drifts in the Bear Creek Summit area often keep it closed even into July. The third option is to take Three-Creek Road along the Nevada/Utah border, which turns south into the Jarbidge Mountains. This route is paved except for the last 18-miles that winds into Jarbidge, deep in the 113,167-acre Jarbidge Wilderness, one of the least frequented wilderness areas in the nation.

So why is it so remote? After all, who would want to start a town in a canyon in the middle of nowhere? Jarbidge got its start around the turn of the century after a local rancher claimed to have found gold in the area. Word began to spread fast about gold in the hills, and shortly after, two men seeking gold and fortune entered Jarbidge Canyon. They allegedly found a cave guarded by a skeleton. After entering the cave both men became extremely ill, forcing them to leave the area and seek treatment. One man died and the other never returned and refused to talk about what happened. This later became the "Lost Sheepherder Mine" legend. By 1909 tales of gold in the hills proved to be true and prospectors flocked to the area. It was one of the last gold rushes of the Old West. Jarbidge became a boomtown practically over night.

Jarbidge is known for a few curious things. It was the location of the last stage robbery in the United States. In 1916 Ben Kuhl and his accomplice, Ed Beck, attacked and killed a man by the name of Fred Searcy as he was driving a horse-drawn stage into Jarbidge. Kuhl and Beck fled with several thousand dollars, but were apprehended and quickly tried. During the robbery, Kuhl left a bloody hand-print on a piece of mail that directly linked him to the murder. This was a new and revolutionary technique for proving guilt, as just six years earlier the first murder conviction using a fingerprint happened in Illinois when Thomas Jennings was convicted after his fingerprints were found at his victim's house. But what Jarbidge is most known for is its namesake — the Jarbidge Giant.

Jarbidge comes from the Shoshone word *Tsawhawbitts* (Tuh saw haw bits). It was thought that *Tsawhawbitts* meant "Devil," but their word for Devil is "Thaw-up." Tsawhawbitts means "Giant" or "monster that lives in the canyon," referring to a belief among local tribes that the canyon was home to a cannibalistic giant. In many Native traditions these names can refer to both an individual creature (like a proper name) and also a group of creatures. So in some tales Tsawhawbitts is a particular individual giant, while in others the name refers to a group of creatures.

The name was difficult for prospectors to say, so they pronounced it Ja-ha-bich (or Johrbitch). When it came time to officially name the district a group of prospectors got together for a meeting to designate the official name. The correct Indian spelling did not appeal favorably to the miners, as they believed its "inelegant combination of letters might offend the public" because the ending of the word Johrbitch might seem vulgar. The majority concluded that the name should be spelled "as to convey the same meaning and look and sound more elegant," so they decided to anglicize the word to Jarbidge. I find it amusing they were more concerned about the name containing "bitch" than they were about naming their community after a cannibalistic monster.

Cannibals of the Canyon

In 1910 Jarbidge merchants, J.M Hawthorne and George C. Riddle, attempted to interview Shoshone Indians about a local legend linked to Jarbidge Valley, though they found the Shoshones exceedingly reluctant to talk about it, and they were overcome with fear whenever the subject was mentioned. The Shoshone make it a point to avoid the Jarbidge area. Eventually Hawthorne found one Shoshone man willing to discuss it, though very reluctantly, and he

refused to give his name, as he was afraid others of his tribe would find out he had told their closely guarded secret.

The Shoshone man said the Tsawhawbitts were huge 30-foot-tall cannibal giants. He picked up a dish pan at hand and said, "Ears big like this pan, eyes big as my hand," while doubling up his fists to illustrate size. According to the Native speaker the Tsawhawbitts become terribly enraged by the sight of fire. Whenever Indians would build fires across the canyon the Tsawhawbitts would roar so loud it would "make the earth shake," they could cross rivers with a single step, and throw stones the size of a man's head great distances at the fire builders. He continued, stating the giants were cannibals that lived by eating human flesh. The Tsawhawbitts were cunning. They would lure Indians into the canyon by making a cooing sound, like a dove. Once they caught someone the giants would throw them into a large basket they carried on their back and bring them back to their cave, believed to be inside a crater near Mt. Ichabod and also near a peak called *Coapiccan Kahni,* meaning "Giant's House." According to the speaker the Tsawhawbitts would "eat 'em, all but the thigh bones. Make fine glue out'n thigh bones." Hawthrone's companion, George C. Riddle, interviewed a Paiute man and received virtually the same story.

It was widely believed the Tsawhawbitts had supernatural powers. Stories mention the Tsawhawbitts having red glowing eyes they would use to hypnotize or paralyze their victims. One look at their eyes and the unfortunate victim would be trapped and unable to move or flee. Then the Tsawhawbitts could easily scoop them up and throw them in their basket — an easy dinner.

A number of Indians from various tribes had entered the canyon but were never heard from again. Only one Indian lived to escape the Tsawhawbitts. He went into the canyon to strip bark off of saplings to fashion bow strings and tent strings. When he lit a fire the Tsawhawbitts went into a rage. He immediately put out his fire and fled for his life into the darkness. The speaker said the story is well known among his tribe at Duck Valley, about 25-miles from Jarbidge Canyon. He had heard this from the oldest Indian of the tribe when he was a boy. Another legend states that a number of Indians once entered the canyon but never returned. It was thought that a volcano erupted in the canyon and killed the party. The area is full of dangerous lava tubes. With all these tales of monsters and tragedy it's no wonder the canyon was generally avoided by the indigenous people.

The area is full of tales of cannibal giants. Shoshone tribe also have tales of *Dzo'avits,* another cannibal giant, and to the north in the Sawtooth Mountains lurked yet another similar giant called *Tso'apittse.* It was said to also be a cannibal and would snatch people with his sticky hands. Their hands were so sticky when they grabbed someone they could pull away their scalp. They also had conical baskets lined with sticky pitch so that victims would get stuck and be unable to escape. Or perhaps they used the glue made from human thigh bones, like the Tsawhawbitts. It was also believed that they had a supernatural power similar to that of the Tsawhawbitts. They were able to put a spell over children that would fix them to the spot, though it didn't work on adults.

These stories are strikingly similar to European Alpine tales of Krampus, a horned and devilish-looking creature that makes his rounds on the night of December 5th. He's the bad counterpart to St. Nicholas. Children leave out their shoes on St. Nicholas Eve (December 5th). If they've been good St. Nicholas will leave a small gift in their shoes; however, if they've been bad Krampus will show up instead. He will snatch the naughty child, put him in a basket he carries on his back, and carry the child off, never to be seen again. In many Krampus tales it's implied that Krampus eats the children. Stories of Krampus are used to scare children into being good.

It's a common theme. Tribes in the Northwest have tales of *Dzunukwa*, the "Basket Woman", a giant cannibalistic ogress that steals naughty children by putting them in her basket to dine on later. One wonders if tales of Tso'apittse and these other basket-carrying monsters were used in a similar way by indigenous people to keep children from wandering into dangerous areas.

At bit to the southwest near Lovelock, the Paiute tribe also has tales of the *Si-Te-Cah*, red-haired giants sometimes described as cannibals. According to Paiute oral history, they used to war with the Si-Te-Cah. After many battles the Si-Te-Cah were finally driven into Lovelock Cave where they were all exterminated. The Paiutes knew they were no match for the giants in close combat, so they built a large fire at mouth of the cave and burned them out.

The word Si-Tech-Cah means "tule eaters" in Paiute. Tule is a fibrous water plant. According to Paiute legends the Si-Ta-Cah would spend time on large rafts of woven tule in Lake Humboldt to escape harassment from the Paiutes.

The Legacy of Jarbidge

Over ten million dollars in gold and silver was extracted from the canyon over the years, but like all boomtowns, eventually Jarbidge went bust. After reaching its peak of around 1500 people in 1911 it began a decline after the mines ceased to be productive. The Elkoro Mining Company bought up most of the claims in Jarbidge until it finally closed operations in the 1930s, leaving

behind 90 thousand feet of abandoned underground mining operations. Today Jarbidge is considered a "living ghost town" and has about 116 residents, mostly those who enjoy its extreme seclusion and isolation.

Interestingly, Jarbidge has a reputation for paranormal activity and peculiar encounters. Paranormal enthusiasts visiting Jarbidge often claim to see mysterious balls of light that appear out of nowhere, zip up into the air, and disappear. The area is also known for alleged Bigfoot activity. If there was ever a place in the country that's big, wild, and remote enough to hide man-eating giants, the 110,000 acres of the Jarbidge Wilderness would be it. Is it possible the cannibalistic Tsawhawbitts was some kind of Bigfoot or Sasquatch creature (or families of creatures) that lived in the cave systems of the canyon? Some Shoshone still won't camp in the canyon to this day, for fear of the giants. Perhaps the giants are still there today, hiding deep in the canyon-lands and cleverly avoiding detection. Except when they want to be seen.

A Jarbidge Encounter

One recent witness, a "Mr. C." from Reno, Nevada, claims he saw a Sasquatch-like creature while camping in the Jarbidge Wilderness in 2015. He shared his compelling encounter on the website *Nevada Sasquatch,* a site "devoted to the exploration of the possibility of an undiscovered bipedal homonid species, making the Silver State their home." In his report titled "BIGFOOT: Hunters Encounter An Aggressive Group of Sasquatch in the Jarbidge Mountains of Northern Nevada," he describes having a frightening encounter at his remote campsite. While in his tent at night he began hearing large footsteps walking around his campsite. Then something started throwing small rocks and debris at his tent and making strange noises. He had the impression there was more than one. This went on for nearly two hours as he sat terrified in the dark. Eventually the disturbing noises and pelting of small rocks stopped. Finally, he gathered the courage to leave the tent, hoping the mysterious creatures had gone. In the light of his flashlight he could see that the mud around the campsite was full of large humanoid footprints with claws coming off the toes. A large branch of a tree had been broken off 11-feet from the ground. He immediately went to wake up his father in another tent and informed him about what had been happening. But as soon as they left the tent to investigate, more small rocks began sailing into the camp from the darkness. They both ran to their truck and drove out of there amid a hail of stones.

The next morning, they returned to the site to retrieve their camping equipment. While packing things up some movement caught Mr. C's eye about 35-yards away. He looked up to the low ridge line and was shocked by what he saw. "I'm staring at a Sasquatch who is staring straight back at me." He continued,

> "It lasted about 4 seconds and then ran up hill into the ravine. This thing was fast and always stayed really low to the ground. It had a burnt auburn, cinnamon colored hair that covered everything I saw on it which was from mid torso on up. It had thinner looking hair on the chest and thicker on the arms. I would have to guess the length at 4, maybe 5 inches. The face had a wide smashed down looking nose with piercing dark eyes that looked recessed back into the head more than you or me. The exposed skin on the face was lighter colored than the hair with a slightly darker buckskin kind of coloration. It didn't have a mustache and had a low wide mouth and jaw line that seemed very robust with a slight conical shaped head that seemed to come directly out of the shoulders with no visible neck. It had very wide shoulders that were probably two or more of me with very large pectoral muscles. This was definitely a male."

Then the creature turned and took off through the sagebrush. Before it vanished out of sight he noted, "I did see a hand when it turned to leave. It swung its left arm up above the ridgeline and you could clearly see a five fingered hand that was quite large." He estimated it was between 7-8 feet tall. Previously Mike was a skeptic, but his astonishing encounter in the Jarbidge Wilderness made him a believer. So if you decide to make the long trek out to the Jabridge Wilderness for some hardcore camping or hiking, make sure to be aware of your surroundings, or you may end up inside the basket of a man-eater.

Resources and Works Consulted:

Mathias, Donald. *A Place Called Jarbidge*. 1997.

Nevada Sasquatch. "BIGFOOT: Hunters Encounter An Aggressive Group of Sasquatch in the Jarbidge Mountains of Northern Nevada." https://nevadasasquatch.blogspot.com/2015/05/bigfoot-hunters-encounter-agressive.html. 2015.

Leigh, Heather. *Haunted Southern Nevada Ghost Towns*. 2022.

"Rush to Camp at Jarbidge Revives Old Indian Legend." *The Idaho Statesman*. February 26, 1910.

"Jarbidge Indian Camp Legend: Why the Miners spelled the name wrong". *Payette Enterprise*. March, 17, 1910.

Smith, Anne M. *Shoshone Tales*. 1993.

Strain, Kathy Moskowitz. *Giants, Cannibals, and Monsters: Bigfoot in Native Culture*. 2020.

Weatherly, David. *Silver State Monsters: Cryptids & Legends of Nevada*. 2019.

Ghost Town Gazetteer

Grafton, Utah

By David Weatherly

Tucked away in Washington County in southern Utah, the ghost town of Grafton lies just south of Zion National Park. There's a good chance that you've had a glimpse of Grafton. It's reportedly the most photographed ghost town in the west and the old schoolhouse is widely recognized.

The site itself was first settled in 1859 as part of a cotton growing project organized by Mormon leader Brigham Young. The first community on the spot was named Wheeler but it didn't last long, being destroyed by a week-long flood in 1862. The settlement was rebuilt a mile upriver and renamed New Grafton after Grafton, Massachusetts.

The town never really boomed. According to historical documents, there were some twenty-eight families in Grafton in 1864 but the community faced major issues. Grafton was isolated, meaning there was no extended community. Grafton farmers soon discovered that raising crops was especially difficult. The Virgin River dumped so much silt into the irrigation canals that they had to be dredged out on a weekly basis just to keep water going to the crops. When the Black Hawk War broke out in 1866, residents abandoned the site and moved to the town of Rockville for safety. After hostilities ended, few people returned to the town and by 1890 only four families remained in Grafton. The last residents finally left in 1944 and in 1946, the town was purchased by Hollywood producer Harry Sherman who wanted to use it as a film location.

If you're a fan of western movies, some of Grafton's buildings will certainly look familiar—the town has been used in several films including 1929's *In Old Arizona*, the first "talkie" to be filmed outside.

Grafton's old schoolhouse is often recognized for its appearance in the 1969 hit *Butch Cassidy and the Sundance Kid.* The film starred Paul Newman and Robert Redford and told the story of the famous outlaw duo. The movie has been rated one of the top 100 greatest American films by the American Film Institute and was selected for preservation in the United States Film Registry in 2003.

In 1997, the Grafton Heritage Partnership stepped in to oversee the protection and preservation of the historic town.

There's something else about Grafton as well—not only is it a ghost town, but it's also said to *have* ghosts. Several reports of paranormal activity have come from the town's old cemetery where investigators have heard disembodied voices, odd sounds, and have had pebbles thrown at them by unseen assailants.

Some might assume that any experiences can be attributed to the "creepy ghost town" atmosphere, but there were definitely recorded deaths in the short-lived community. The infant mortality rate was high with numerous children passing away before the age of one. A nine-year-old boy named Joseph Field was dragged to death by a horse, and there were deaths due to tuberculosis. Perhaps these tragedies led to residual hauntings, the recorded impressions of events left on the land. If so, it could explain some of the various reports. Witnesses have heard the ghostly cries of children, disembodied voices talking and laughing around the buildings, and one witness claims to have heard a woman scream while he was exploring the town. The most interesting report comes from a couple who said they saw the phantom of a woman walking near the old schoolhouse.

Ghosts or not, the historic town of Grafton is well worth a stop when exploring southern Utah.

Resources and Works Consulted:

www.Graftonheritage.org

I Dare You!

True Love Lives in Central City

By Chad Lewis

When we think of historic wild west states, Colorado is often overlooked for the more traditional southwestern desert states. Perhaps the numerous snow-covered mountain ranges and beautiful plateaus mislead us and force us to forget that the landscape of Colorado is more diverse than just having the Rocky Mountains. The wild grass-covered plains of the state are especially amazing, and are more in line with what people tend to think of as the wild west. Regardless of what you think of The Centennial State, it is home to one of the sweetest (and weirdest) dares that you will find.

Tucked a bit west of the Denver metro area is the historic mining town of Central City. Settled in 1859, the town soon was flooded with gold rush prospectors. Due to the overabundance of gold, at one point the city was known as "the richest square mile on earth." The days when miners overflowed the streets are long gone, and the wild rowdy days seem like a fanciful distant memory. Today, the historic town houses a population of nearly 800 residents. Two residents that you will not find among the living are those of John Cameron and the mysterious mourning specter that visits his grave.

The haunted legend goes something like this. Outside of town is the Central City Masonic Cemetery. Perched atop a large knoll, the tall grass-covered boneyard looks like something out of a dusty spaghetti western film. Inside the cemetery is the old grave of John Cameron. Little is known about the former resident. His gravestone lists his date of death as being November 1, 1887. He was only 21 at the time of his death, the cause of which has been lost to history. Most likely he was one of the countless miners who made their way to the gold city looking to strike it rich. Perhaps he was a store owner, all too glad to sell prospectors everything they needed for their quest. The only thing that remains clear is that at least one unidentified woman was terribly distraught over his death. So distraught, in fact, that every year on the anniversary of his death, this unknown woman, dressed in a long, black Victorian era dress, rises from her grave and brings flowers to her lover.

The dare tells that if you visit John's grave on the date of his death—November 1—or on April 5—you will encounter the ghostly spirit of a woman placing flowers at the deceased man's gravesite. (November 1, which begins just after midnight on Halloween, is also known as All Souls Day but the significance of the April 5 date is unknown.)

The ghostly woman looks as though she stepped right out of another time. Adorned in a pitch-black floor-length gown that one may have worn at an 1800s funeral, the silent mourner lovingly places a bouquet of flowers on his grave. Those who try to gain a closer look at this unknown lady often discover that she vanishes right into thin air. Just as the background and history of Mr. Cameron is unknown, the identity of this visiting suitor remains a mystery. The main legend tells of her being Mr. Cameron's heartbroken sweetheart or wife, who refuses to allow death to come between her and her true love. Others speculate that the black clad woman was actually Mr. Cameron's mistress, and to avoid detection from his wife or other nosy residents, she slinks into the cemetery only under the cover of darkness. In 2006, the *Fort Collins Coloradoan* described the woman's dress as being made of satin.

The success of dares is largely based upon your completing them on a specific date or exact time. Usually these correspond to the anniversary of an untimely death, accident, murder, or suicide. The belief is that this type of tragedy, which is usually associated with hauntings, monsters, and curses, releases such powerful emotions that it leaves a permanent supernatural scar on the landscape. With this in mind, I hope the vanishing woman in black rewards you for showing up to see her.

Resources and Works Consulted:

Fort Collins Coloradoan. October 22, 2006.

Fort Collins Coloradoan. October 23, 2011.

Disclaimer

The "I Dare You" column and its challenges are presented for educational and entertainment purposes only. The authors, publisher, and Back Roads Lore will not be liable for any injury to, or death of, any persons or for the damage to, or destruction or loss of any items or property, whether caused by gross negligence of the owners, its employees, agents, contractors, or any other persons, or for any other reasons associated with this publication.

Dedication

This volume is dedicated to:

Ambrose Bierce (June 24, 1842 – c. 1914)

Writer, journalist, soldier, and adventurer

Ambrose Gwinnett Bierce was born in a log cabin at Horse Cave Creek in Meigs County, Ohio, on June 24, 1842. At 15 he left home to work as a "printer's devil" (a young apprentice in a printing shop) at a small abolitionist newspaper, the *Northern Indianan*. It was here that Bierce acquired his love for journalism and a good story.

At the start of the American Civil War, Bierce enlisted in the Union Army's 9th Indiana Infantry. He received high praise for his daring rescue of a gravely injured comrade, while under heavy fire, at the Battle of Rich Mountain. He also fought at the Battle of Shiloh. The terrifying experience left a deep impression on Bierce and became a source for several short stories and the memoir "What I Saw of Shiloh." In June of 1864, Bierce sustained a traumatic brain injury at the Battle of Kennesaw Mountain, an injury that would trouble him for the rest of his life, resulting in episodes of fainting and irritability. In 1866 he joined an expedition to inspect military outposts across the Great Plains, traveling mostly by horseback from Omaha to San Francisco. Bierce was awarded the rank of brevet major before resigning from the Army to continue his career in journalism.

Bierce remained in San Francisco for a number of years, eventually becoming famous as a contributor and editor of newspapers and periodicals. In 1879 his love for adventure got the better of him, and he moved to Deadwood in the Dakota Territory and accepted a job as a manager for a mining company. After the company failed he returned to San Francisco to resume his writing career. Between 1888 and 1893 he wrote most of his most famous works, including the satirical work *The Devil's Dictionary*, the tale "An Occurrence at Owl Creek Bridge," and *Can Such Things Be?*, a collection of superb supernatural horror tales. Bierce became one of the most prominent and influential writers and journalists on the West Coast and one of the early pioneers of the psychological horror story.

In 1913 Bierce (then aged 71) traveled to Mexico to cover the Mexican Revolution. In Ciudad Juárez he joined Pancho Villa's army as an observer — what we would call a war correspondent today. While riding with Poncho Villa he witnessed the Battle of Tierra Blanca. Shortly after, Ambrose Bierce vanished without a trace. His last communication was a letter to a friend that ended with, "As for me, I leave here tomorrow for an unknown destination." He was never seen again. There are many theories and rumors about Bierce's fate. In one of his final letters, he jokingly stated:

"Good-bye. If you hear of my being stood up against a Mexican stone wall and shot to rags, please know that I think it is a pretty good way to depart this life. It beats old age, disease, or falling down the cellar stairs. To be a Gringo in Mexico—ah, that is euthanasia!"

His grim statement is very typical of Bierce's dark humor and wit. Oddly, Bierce's wry comment may have been prophetic, as a priest in Sierra Mojada, Coahuila, claimed that Bierce was executed by firing squad in the town's cemetery, but no body was ever found. The disappearance of Ambrose Bierce remains one of the most famous disappearances in American literary history and one of the most puzzling unsolved mysteries of the Old West. His sense of adventure, journalistic fearlessness, macabre interests, and gallows humor serve as an inspiration for all of us at Back Roads Lore.

Back Roads Lore

Back Roads Lore began as a small collective of like-minded researchers with a simple mission—to chronicle anomalous events, Fortean mysteries, urban legends, and strange folklore. As the name implies, we put special emphasis on legends that are off the beaten track, but we don't shy away from high strangeness wherever it's found.

The individuals that are part of Back Roads Lore have put in decades of research and have traveled the world to unearth curious legends, but they don't rest! Exploring is an essential component of the work and with rare exception, we always make sure to visit the actual locations of the legends we investigate. One of the core tenets of Back Roads Lore is to get out there and experience these legendary and infamous places firsthand. It also allows us the opportunity to interview witnesses and locals and to better understand the perspectives of those personally affected by strange events. We aim to minimize so-called "armchair research," as there is no substitute for actual field experience and on-site observation. Such an approach also opens the door for countless adventures as we take deep dives into lost legends and weirdness.

It's not our goal to prove or disprove the existence of unusual creatures, cryptids, ghosts, aliens, or anything else. Rather, we prefer to present the facts, history, and lore, along with critical analysis, so that readers can make up their own mind and decide what they believe.

Amazing stories speak for themselves, but Back Roads Lore also examines new theories and unconventional concepts as we try to understand the deeper level of the strange events that happen in our world.

Lastly, many local legends and curious bits of regional lore are at risk of vanishing within a generation if they are not recorded and preserved. In the past, people kept unusual local tales alive mostly through oral traditions, often through storytelling at the local tavern or by passing strange cautionary tales down to their children.

Unfortunately, in today's highly mobile society and increasingly isolated culture, most people are generally unaware of the colorful and rich folklore of their own area. Unique history and folklore is something that should be documented and celebrated, as they play an important part of our cultural heritage.

Therefore, it is our hope that Back Roads Lore will fulfill a necessary role by discovering endangered lore and preserving it for future generations.

— Back Roads Lore

David Weatherly is known as the renaissance man of the strange and supernatural. Author, adventurer, magician and more, he has traveled the world in search of mysteries. From dusty castles to strange, remote islands and ancient sites, he has journeyed to the most unusual places on the globe seeking the unknown.

Kevin Lee Nelson is an author, researcher, and adventurer. He has written and lectured on topics of the paranormal, folklore, and the occult for over twenty years. A nomad at heart, Kevin spends much of his time roaming America's back roads in his black muscle car, hunting down strange legends and mysterious encounters.

Chad Lewis is an author, researcher, and lecturer on topics of the strange and unusual. With an academic background in the field of psychology, Chad has traveled the world in search of the supernatural. The more bizarre the legend is, the more likely you will find Chad there.

Printed in Dunstable, United Kingdom

76896704R00093